Caring Like Jesus
The Matthew 18 Project

Daniel Ulrich
Janice Fairchild

Brethren Press®

Caring Like Jesus: The Matthew 18 Project

Copyright 2002 by Daniel Ulrich and Janice Fairchild.

Published by Brethren Press, 1451 Dundee Avenue, Elgin, Illinois 60120. Brethren Press is a program of the Church of the Brethren General Board.

06 05 04 03 02   5 4 3 2 1

Library of Congress Control Number: 2002106065

Manufactured in the United States of America

To David and Paula,
who made this book possible
with many quiet gifts of patience and love.

Contents

Preface

One of the promises in Matthew 18 is an incentive for Jesus' disciples to agree with one another: "If two of you agree on earth about anything you ask, it will be done for you by my Father in heaven" (18:19). The authors of this book often claimed that promise as we journeyed from an initial idea to a finished manuscript. We share a deep concern for the mission of Christ's church, including the essential work of reconciliation within and beyond the church. After teaching about Matthew 18 together, we agreed that a book on Matthew 18 and its context could be useful for disciples who seek to follow Jesus faithfully in the twenty-first century. We agreed that this book should combine several elements: careful attention to the biblical story, current stories about people who have tried to practice the values taught in Matthew 18, and practical suggestions for readers who wanted to practice those values more fully.

We agreed that the book should be a collaborative effort and that we would invite others to participate by contributing stories. We agreed to practice Matthew 18 in our working relationship by listening carefully, speaking frankly, striving for consensus, and offering our agreements to God as prayers.

Now, as this book goes to press, we celebrate the many ways in which our prayers have been answered. We received many inspiring stories. Working together has been a joy. We resolved our small disagreements quickly, and we found efficient ways to share the work. (Jan took the lead in gathering stories and in writing the "Story Starters" and study questions. Dan wrote the "Biblical Story" sections and pulled together most of the "Our Stories" sections.) Although we live two thousand miles apart, we exchanged drafts instantly by e-mail, and each improved the other's writing.

God has also answered our prayers through the help of many other people, only some of whom we can mention here. Financial support for collaborative research and writing came through a generous summer grant from the Wabash Center for Teaching and Learning in Theology and Religion. The trustees of Bethany Theological Seminary supported Dan's work on this project by granting a four-month sabbatical. Marcia Shetler, Bethany's director of public relations, helped prepare and distribute a brochure requesting stories. Bob Gross, Dan McFadden, and Barb Sayler were especially helpful in alerting us to stories they had encountered. Jan's husband, David Fairchild, reviewed the manuscript and made many valuable suggestions. Most of all, we are grateful for the people who took the time to share stories with us. There was only enough space to publish some of them, but we learned from them all.

Many of the stories included here are about congregations or individuals in the Church of the Brethren. That bias came naturally since both authors are Brethren and since we relied on church connections in our search for stories. Even so, we hope that readers from other denominations (or no denomination) will find this book worthwhile. The joys and struggles described here are not unique to any church body, and honest storytelling can help to show how much we have in common. Partly as an orientation for readers from other traditions, we have included a chapter on how Matthew 18 has been interpreted in the history of the Church of the Brethren. That history helps to explain why we are so passionate about one chapter in the Bible and why we believe that a new interpretation is needed. Although we begin with the past, our purpose is to interpret Matthew 18 for the current and future life of the church.

Looking to the future, we hope this book will lead to more stories of faithful discipleship. As you read and discuss it, you may remember other people who have lived out the values taught in Matthew 18. Perhaps a new story will emerge from your own attempts to live those values or from your observation of others. If you feel led to share a brief story, we would be glad to receive it and possibly to post it on the Internet.

Send stories by regular mail to Daniel W. Ulrich, Bethany Theological Seminary, 615 National Road West, Richmond, IN 47374; or by e-mail to ulricda@bethanyseminary.edu. Please include a telephone number and address where you can be reached for confirmation. To read stories that others have contributed, visit www.matthew18project.org. We hope to maintain this web page for at least three years beginning in July 2002.

1

Matthew 18
in the Church of the Brethren

Matthew 18 has been extremely important in the history of the Church of the Brethren. The Brethren movement began among radical Pietists, who had left the established churches of Germany out of a desire to be more obedient to scripture. When they debated whether to start a new church, one of their most convincing arguments was that they needed a church in order to practice Matthew 18:15-20.[1] Matthew 18 has figured in many of the highs and lows of Brethren history. It helped hold the church together during the U.S. Civil War, and it was instrumental in the divisions that took place twenty years later.[2]

For the Church of the Brethren, the heart of Matthew 18 has been the four-step disciplinary process spelled out in verses 15-17. When a member believed another had sinned, the first step was to visit the offender alone in order to explain the situation and ask for repentance. If the offender repented, then the matter was settled. If not, there was a second visit involving one or two others as witnesses. If that visit also failed, then the whole congregation would hear the matter and add its own call for repentance. The last resort was for the congregation to treat the offender as "a Gentile and a tax collector" (18:17), which meant imposing a "ban" or "avoidance" until the offender decided to repent. The Church of the Brethren regularly used this method of discipline from its beginning in 1708 until the early twentieth century. Few congregations now practice discipline in this way, but the memory of it still lingers. Just ask some longtime members what comes to mind when they hear the words "Matthew 18"!

Alexander Mack on Matthew 18

The earliest leader of the Brethren movement, Alexander Mack, Sr., wrote of the "ban" as an ordinance commanded by Christ and thus as a mark of the true church.[3] In "Basic Questions" (1713), Mack explained that the ban did not require cutting off all contact. The offender was not to be treated as an enemy but could still be admonished as a sister or brother. If the banned person was poor or in need, then church members should offer help just as they would to other needy people.[4] Two years later in "Rights and Ordinances," Mack put more emphasis on the church's need to remain pure by separating itself from unrepentant members. Mack acknowledged that all people are guilty of sin, but he drew a sharp distinction between sinners who repented and those who did not. The ban was not a punishment for the original offense, but a necessary response to any member who rejected the church's call for repentance. As biblical support for the ban, Mack interpreted Matthew 18:17 ("let such a one be to you as a Gentile and a tax collector") in light of 1 Corinthians 5:11, where Paul commands believers not to associate with "anyone who bears the name of brother or sister who is sexually immoral or greedy, or is an idolater, reviler, drunkard, or robber. Do not even eat with such a one."[5] Thus, the "ban" and "avoidance" were similar in meaning. When Mack's granddaughter Hannah was banned by the church, her family did not eat with her.[6]

Mack's teaching of "the ban" was part of a larger vision for the church, a vision heavily influenced by Swiss and German Anabaptists. Mack affirmed that all believers should interpret and practice the New Testament together. When believers joined the church through adult baptism, they agreed not only to accept Christ as their Lord and Savior, but also to participate in and abide by the church's decisions about the meaning of scripture. These decisions were never to be fixed in stone, since the church always needed to question its traditions in light of scripture. Members who disagreed with a decision were free to advocate change but not to disobey the decision while it remained in effect.

Two Centuries of Strict Discipline

As Brethren attempted to live out Mack's vision during the next two centuries, Annual Meetings repeatedly decided what actions would or would not be subject to discipline by the church. Some of these decisions still seem important, such as those forbidding slave ownership or participation in war. Others may seem trivial now, such as many of the regulations defining plain dress and setting limits on conformity with the world. Regardless of the issue, Annual Meeting minutes often ended with a warning that any member who did not abide with this decision would be dealt with "according to Matthew 18."[7] The writers of these minutes would undoubtedly have affirmed that believers should practice *all* of Matthew 18, including its emphasis on humility, compassion, and unlimited forgiveness. Nevertheless, one gets the impression that "according to Matthew 18" had become a short-hand way to threaten expulsion for disobedient members. "Matthew 18" meant specifically verses 15-17.

In many ways this tendency to isolate verses 15-17 from their context is not surprising. Whenever a passage of scripture is especially treasured by the church, it is also especially vulnerable to being taken out of context. Members quote the passage often but forget to mention how it fits within the larger writing. Eventually the passage takes on a life of its own. Such has been the fate of Matthew 18:15-17 in the Church of the Brethren.

By the middle of the nineteenth century, the church's disciplinary rules had become increasingly complex. In 1842, Annual Meeting defined degrees of avoidance depending on the seriousness of the original offense. Complete avoidance was reserved for serious offenses "against God and the truth" such as those named by Paul in 1 Corinthians 5:9-11.[8] Other offenses required only partial avoidance, which meant exclusion from the holy kiss, church council, and love feast (which included feetwashing, a meal, and communion). At baptism every member pledged to cooperate with the church's practice of discipline according to Matthew 18. If members disobeyed the church's decision to avoid someone, then they were also subject to avoidance.[9]

Deacons and elders carried much of the responsibility for disciplining members within their congregations, and elders could also jointly discipline members of other congregations. Deacons and elders regularly visited members who were thought to be guilty of some offense. Deacons also made annual visits to every family in a congregation, asking whether the family was at peace with all others in the church. Any grievances had to be worked out before the members involved could attend love feast. One elderly brother recalled that "they would really hunt for something to straighten out [chuckles]. I don't think I'm exaggerating."[10]

Nineteenth-century church records are full of references to "trials," "witnesses," "testimony," and "convictions."[11] These records sound quite legalistic, partly because they focus on difficult cases that could not be resolved privately. Most cases were probably resolved before they reached a congregation's records, and much effective pastoral care took place through efforts to practice Matthew 18. On the other hand, there were also many cases in which the church's discipline was neither loving nor redemptive.[12]

Twentieth-Century Changes

One story of redemptive discipline involves the church trial of Elder David G. Wine, which took place in 1920. Wine's grandson Berwyn Oltman tells it in this way:

> Elder Wine, a pioneer preacher in western Nebraska, had a vision for developing the agricultural potential of the land in the area in which he helped to establish a Brethren congregation. When two brothers from eastern Kansas were looking for land, Wine encouraged them by letter and eventually helped them locate in the community. After a year of drought and crop failure, the disillusioned brothers accused Wine of "misrepresentation." In good Brethren fashion, he chose not to have a lawyer, and a district court convicted him of mail fraud.
>
> Wine's accusers also tried to convince the Enders Church of the Brethren that he should not continue as an elder. At a special council meeting, the church agreed to accept the decision of three visiting elders. The elders interviewed all who had been involved, including Wine's accusers and many church members who had believed them. The elders determined that Wine had been completely honest, but that he should have been more patient with his accusers. Once they had come to Wine while he was repairing a fence, and he said, "If it weren't for the grace of God, I would surely strike you with this hammer." Wine apologized before the church for the remark, adding "That was really true, but I should not have said it."
>
> A local pastor, Virgil C. Finnell, had believed the accusations against Wine without investigating them himself. After hearing the facts brought out by the committee, Finnell admitted that he

had been wrong and that he had gone so far as to write many Brethren telling them the awful things that Wine had done. He was told that he must write every one of them and correct the error. Many church members came to Wine later and with tears confessed their wrong in doubting his integrity.

Wine's accusers were not reconciled with him, and for a time they left the church. The peace of the congregation, however, was maintained. After a few months in prison, Wine returned to pastor the congregation for the remainder of his life. He insisted that his family should not hold any ill will toward the people who had accused him. When Wine's oldest daughter married the son of one of the accusers, the circle of reconciliation was complete.[13]

Wine's church trial is exceptional both because he was innocent of the charges and because he repented of his real sin of "impatience."

Unfortunately, church trials in the early twentieth century were rarely so redemptive. Often the accused was neither innocent nor repentant, and sometimes the accusers were just as guilty as the accused. Carl Bowman's interviews with older members of the Church of the Brethren provide several examples:

> After I was a minister, there was a couple of girls that was wearing hats, and with that, going to places of amusements, so that the church had 'em up before a council meeting . . . and they were disfellowshipped. . . . And eh, well, I didn't have any part of it—I was just a listener. And the girls went out swimming soon after they were disfellowshipped and one of 'em drowned in the lake. And they had an older brother, and many, many years afterwards, he blamed me for having part in their disfellowshipping. . . . I couldn't take that blame because I was too young and didn't take any part of the older people. . . .
>
> And I didn't believe in that. In my time, I don't know as we ever disfellowshipped anyone after I became elder. I don't remember we ever did. . . . I think in the church today, generally speaking, there's more Christianity than there was when we were made to do those things.[14]

———

When I was at Narrow Spring, we had a Sister in the congregation, and it was common knowledge she was a prostitute. I remember as a pastor going to visit her and periodically she'd feign illness, etc., and finally one of the deacons came to me and said, "John, you don't know the situation there; she's a prostitute; she just wants a man there." I thanked him and thereafter I never went to visit her unless I took my wife along or a deacon. So, finally this became common knowledge in the community that she was a prostitute, and we discussed it at Official Board and we just felt that it wasn't a good influence, so we counseled with her, and counseled with her. She denied the thing and everybody knew what was going on, so finally the church disowned her, disfellowshipped her. She had two sisters in the church; they became inactive after that. My attitude was, "from now on I'm not going to be part of any disowning."

. . . That changed my feeling and I think my feeling was typical of a lot of others, particularly the pastors who came in. . . . I just felt that the church is not for perfect people, and we need to be more understanding and more helpful and more compassionate. Even to this day, I somehow have sort of a guilty feeling that we didn't do as much as we should have to help the woman.[15]

———

The Hill Church picnic [non-Brethren] was a very exciting social event, and the young people from all over that area went there. . . . How the Official Board ever discovered the names of the young people who went there is beyond me, but I tell you, there was a lot of tattling going on . . . and they would report this to some deacon or some minister, and many times then the individual would be visited. "Is this true that you were there?" And if they admitted that it was true, then they would say, "Well, we ask you to appear at the next Council Meeting to make a confession." Sometimes you had a whole row of them would confess that they had gone. The time came when they wouldn't admit that they were sorry; they would simply say, "We're sorry we offended the church," so that was the last. . . . I just felt that many times the older Brethren asked questions and went into areas in which they had absolutely no business. It was purely personal.[16]

These stories help explain why official church discipline had become rare by the 1930s.[17] To some extent, the decline in discipline was due to a rise in individualism. The Church of the Brethren was rapidly changing from a German sect into an American denomination. North American culture was becoming more individualistic, and liberal Brethren increasingly accepted the idea that members should make up their own minds about how to dress and (to some extent) how to live.[18] Nevertheless, individualism does not fully explain the decline in official discipline. Too often, the church had acted without enough humility, compassion, and forgiveness. In other words, while the church was zealously practicing Matthew 18:15-17, it was neglecting the rest of the chapter. Whenever discipline was practiced without the other values emphasized in Matthew 18, it tended to alienate both the offender and anyone else who had compassion on the offender. That experience of alienation influenced many leaders to reject church discipline altogether.

Unfortunately, the decline in official discipline did not automatically increase members' compassion or decrease alienation. Unofficial avoidance based on gossip could be even more devastating than the official variety. The "offender" might never hear what others think happened and might never have a chance to tell the other side of the story. Avoidance might be continued long after he or she had repented. In contrast, official discipline was supposed to end whenever the offender apologized before the congregation. At that point each member of the congregation was told to welcome back the offender with a kiss of peace and never to speak of the matter again.[19] An obvious alternative to gossip was to do and say nothing about others' sins, but silence was not compassionate in the long run either. It could not always be maintained, and it did nothing to help people who were suffering because of their own sins or the sins of others.

Probably the most far-reaching drawback to the decline of official discipline was a weakening in the church's sense of identity. The Church of the Brethren had become alienated from an important part of its heritage. Annual Conference continued to speak for the church, but members could simply choose not to listen. Wide differences in belief and practice made it more difficult to define what it meant to be a member of Church of the Brethren.

During the second half of the twentieth century, these concerns moved some church leaders to call for a renewed practice of Matthew 18.[20] One important call came in the 1976 Annual Conference statement on "Discipleship and Reconciliation." It lists the failure to resolve differences according to Matthew 18 as one of the causes of brokenness in the church, and it urges all members to follow a process for reconciliation modeled after Matthew 18:15-17. The comments on the fourth step in verse 17 are especially interesting:

> After all efforts have been exhausted and reconciliation cannot occur or the person refuses to be in fellowship and harmony with the corporate body, the action counseled in Matthew 18:17 may be necessary.
>
> The biblical teaching of Matthew 18, traditionally practiced in the Church of the Brethren, can be misinterpreted. It can be insensitively and hastily employed. However, when verse seventeen, "let him be to you as a Gentile and a tax collector" (RSV), is understood within the context of the *total* chapter, it reflects the openness and unending compassion of Jesus. Gentiles and tax collectors . . . as well as other rejected persons were the focus of his compassion and forgiveness (Matthew 9:9; 21:28-32; Luke 5:28-32; 7:24-50; 15:3-32; 18:9-14; 19:1-10; and John 4:7-26; 8:3-11).[21]

This statement is remarkable for several reasons: It avoids the word *discipline*; it revises the traditional Brethren interpretation of Matthew 18:17; and it emphasizes the context of that verse. The statement does not explore the context in much depth, but it certainly points in that direction.

Since the adoption of the 1976 Annual Conference statement, many denominational leaders and organizations have promoted Matthew 18 as a guide for resolving conflicts in and beyond the church. Most districts have discipleship and reconciliation committees, which regularly employ Matthew 18 in their work with congregations in conflict. One of the programs of the On Earth Peace Assembly is the Ministry of Reconciliation, which offers "Matthew 18 Workshops" for congregations and other church groups interested in improving their skills in communication and conflict management. The suggested curriculum includes questions about the immediate context of Matthew 18:15-20.

More than twenty congregations in a variety of districts hosted Matthew 18 Workshops in 1998–2000.[22] Finally, the Association of Brethren Caregivers has published a *Deacon Manual for Caring Ministries,* which includes a section on "Unity and Reconciliation Ministries." The manual urges deacons to apply Matthew 18:15-17, while listening actively and compassionately to those they visit.[23]

The current emphasis on reconciliation and conflict resolution contrasts with earlier uses of Matthew 18. In traditional church discipline, the problem is "sin" and the goal is to admonish and win back the one identified as a sinner. In most mediation training, the problem (and opportunity) is "conflict," and the goal is to reach an agreement in which everyone benefits. Mediators try to avoid labeling one party to a conflict as the sinner. Of course, sin and conflict often go hand in hand, and clear communication is important in dealing with both. Therefore, church discipline and conflict resolution are related.

Although conflict resolution is popular now, some leaders have called for a return to the language of "sin" and "discipline." In 1993, the Brethren Revival Fellowship published "A Biblical Study of Church Discipline." This article cites Matthew 18:15-17 and other isolated verses for support. It calls for "admonition" when a member sins, "disassociation" if the member fails to repent after two warnings, and "restoration" if the member repents. An accompanying editorial refers to the rest of Matthew 18 and emphasizes the need for "simple humility," "frank honesty," "united prayer," and a "forgiving spirit" when carrying out church discipline.[24]

Although there are important differences among these current interpretations of Matthew 18, there is also much common ground. All agree that the Church of the Brethren needs to renew its practice of Matthew 18 while avoiding the abuses of the past, and most emphasize that Matthew 18:15-17 should be read in context. Both the common ground and the differences point to a need for more study of Matthew 18 in the context of the whole Gospel.

How This Book Fits In
The authors hope this book will be a helpful resource for pastors, deacons, workshop participants, Sunday school classes, and anyone who seeks to follow Jesus more faithfully. Since we want to interpret Matthew 18 in context, the next chapter offers a broad view of the Gospel

in order to clarify the role of Matthew 18 within the story that Matthew tells. In later chapters, we will explore all of Matthew 18, allowing information from the rest of the story to shape our interpretations of the chapter. We will not neglect verses 15-17, but neither will we assume that those verses are more important than the rest. When historical background from the first century seems important to clarify Matthew's meaning, we will mention it as well. We will also illustrate our biblical interpretations with stories that we remember or that others have graciously shared with us.

Our purpose is not to advocate a return to all the ways in which Brethren practiced Matthew 18 in the eighteenth and nineteenth centuries. Even if we could turn back the clock, we would not want to do so. Rather, we advocate a return to scripture and to the God who inspired it. We hope that Matthew 18, studied in context, will speak afresh to our generation, teaching us how to follow Jesus more faithfully in our own times. Although we have begun with a historical survey, the stories presented in later chapters will show that discipleship according to Matthew 18 is not just a thing of the past. With Christ's help, believers can live out the values taught in Matthew 18.

Questions for Discussion

1. What do you think of when you hear "Matthew 18"? How do you feel when you hear, "They need to practice Matthew 18"?
2. What does "church discipline" mean today? Do you believe that congregations should attempt to discipline their members? If so, how? What offenses, if any, require corrective discipline?
3. Before reading this chapter, did you associate other values such as humility, hospitality, and forgiveness with Matthew 18? Why is it important to explore Matthew 18:15-17 in the context of the entire chapter?
4. What is your understanding of mediation training or Matthew 18 Workshops? If you have participated in either of these, or if you have participated in mediation of some kind, share your evaluation of the process and the outcome. How was Matthew 18 interpreted? How was it practiced?

5. Evaluate your congregation's practice of Matthew 18. Are most members aware of Matthew 18? How are members practicing it now? How could that practice improve?

NOTES

1. Alexander Mack, Jr., makes this point in his preface to the first American edition (1774) of the writings of Alexander Mack, Sr. See Donald F. Durnbaugh, ed., *European Origins of the Brethren: A Source Book on the Beginnings of the Church of the Brethren in the Early Eighteenth Century* (Elgin, Ill.: Brethren Press, 1958), 120, 122.

2. Donald F. Durnbaugh, *Fruit of the Vine: A History of the Brethren, 1708–1995* (Elgin, Ill.: Brethren Press, 1997), 265-268, 308-313.

3. Alexander Mack, Sr., "Rights and Ordinances," *The Complete Writings of Alexander Mack*, ed. William R. Eberly (Winona Lake, Ind.: BMH Books, 1991), 63-67.

4. Alexander Mack, Sr., "Basic Questions," *Complete Writings*, 34-35.

5. Mack, "Rights and Ordinances," *Complete Writings*, 63-68.

6. Kenneth M. Shaffer, Jr., and Graydon F. Snyder, *Texts in Transit II* (Elgin, Ill.: Brethren Press, 1991), 46.

7. See, for example, *Minutes of Annual Meetings of the Church of the Brethren Containing All Available Minutes from 1778 to 1909* (Elgin, Ill.: Brethren Publishing House, 1909), 86, 149, 153, 172, 175, 182, 184, 185, 186, 203, 213, 214, 216, 219, 220, 227, 239, 252, 253, 254, 313, 315, 327.

8. *Minutes of Annual Meetings*, 74-75.

9. Carl F. Bowman, *Brethren Society: The Cultural Transformation of a "Peculiar People"* (Baltimore: The Johns Hopkins University Press, 1995), 15, 56, 89-92.

10. Bowman, *Brethren Society*, 192-93, 447 n.16, quoting a personal interview conducted in 1985 with "a one-hundred-year-old Brother from Ohio."

11. Bowman, *Brethren Society*, 92.

12. Shaffer and Snyder, *Texts*, 48.

13. This story was shared by Berwyn L. Oltman in 2000 and has been edited for length. It is based on a journal written by Virginia Wine Snavely at the time of the events.

14. Bowman, *Brethren Society*, 286, quoting an interview with an elderly brother from the southwestern United States" (see p. 458 n. 52). The ellipses are Bowman's. Reprinted with permission of The Johns Hopkins University Press.

15. Bowman, *Brethren Society*, 286-87, quoting an interview with "another brother from the Southwest" (see p. 458 n. 53). Ellipses are Bowman's. Reprinted with permission of The Johns Hopkins University Press.

16. Bowman, *Brethren Society,* 287, quoting an interview with "an eastern Pennsylvania elder." Ellipses are Bowman's. Reprinted with permission of The Johns Hopkins University Press.

17. A 1935 query to Annual Conference from the Hagerstown (Md.) Church of the Brethren complained, "Inasmuch as church discipline, even for gross moral offenses has so nearly disappeared among Protestant bodies, and since the practice of our own church in this regard has become lax and our method of procedure vague and uncertain. . . ." The answer adopted in 1937 affirmed "disciplinary measures (Matt. 18:17)" but did not specifically call for the practice of

avoidance. See *Minutes of Annual Meetings of the Church of the Brethren, 1910–1937* (Elgin: Ill.: Brethren Publishing House, 1937), 7-8.

18. Bowman, *Brethren Society*, 274, 281-89.

19. Shaffer and Snyder, *Texts*, 48.

20. See especially Eugene F. Roop, "Brethren and Church Discipline (I)," 92-102, and "Brethren and Church Discipline (II)," 168-82, *Brethren Life and Thought* 14 (1969); Estella B. Horning, "The Rule of Christ: An Exposition of Matthew 18:15-20," *Brethren Life and Thought* 28 (1993): 69-78. For a Mennonite perspective, see Marlin Jeschke, *Discipling in the Church: Recovering a Ministry of the Gospel*, 3rd ed., rev. and enl. (Scottdale, Pa.: Herald Press, 1988).

21. *Minutes of the Annual Conference of the Church of the Brethren, 1975–1979*, comp. Phyllis Kingery Ruff (Elgin, Ill.: Brethren Press, 1980), 201, 202. Emphasis original.

22. Telephone interview with Robert Gross, September 27, 2000. For further information, contact the On Earth Peace Assembly office at 410-635-8704.

23. Association of Brethren Caregivers, *Deacon Manual for Caring Ministries* (Elgin, Ill.: Association of Brethren Caregivers, 1999), 42-53.

24. Mark Baliles, "A Biblical Study of Church Discipline," *BRF Witness* 28/4 (1993): 5-10; and Harold Martin, "Editorial," *BRF Witness* 28/4 (1993): 2-4.

2

Matthew's Story About Jesus

Complaining about a problem is often easier than solving it. In chapter 1 we complained that Matthew 18:15-17 has sometimes been taken out of context. Here we begin the harder task of taking the context into account. This chapter introduces the Gospel of Matthew as a story told by Christian missionaries. Later, as we explore Matthew 18 in detail, we will continue to refer to the larger historical and literary picture.

Author, Purpose, and Intended Audience

Throughout this book "Matthew" is used as a convenient and traditional name for the human author of the Gospel of Matthew. All four canonical Gospels were originally anonymous, perhaps because the authors wanted to keep their readers' attention focused on Jesus. Titles like "according to Matthew" were added after the Gospels began to circulate together in the second century A.D. The best evidence about the author comes from the Gospel itself, and from comparisons with other Gospels. Based on this evidence, most scholars conclude that the Gospel of Matthew was written in the late first century A.D., by someone who drew on the Gospel of Mark and other sources.

Matthew was very well versed in Jewish traditions and saw Jesus as the fulfillment of all God's promises to Israel.[1] Furthermore, Matthew's vision for the mission of the church went beyond Israel to include all nations. In that regard, Matthew was like Paul, Priscilla, and other Jewish-Christians who actively evangelized Gentiles. Matthew's vision is expressed most clearly in the command to "make disciples of all nations, baptizing them in the name of the Father and of the Son and of the Holy Spirit, and teaching them to obey everything that I have commanded you" (28:19-20). The Greek verb translated "make disciples" in 28:19 has a broad meaning. It includes the tasks that we usually associate with evangelism, such as calling and baptizing new disciples, but it does not stop there. It also includes training, guiding, and modeling—everything a teacher does for a student throughout their time together.

The Gospel of Matthew is a tool for making disciples in the broad sense of the word. Following the pattern of other ancient biographers, Matthew was not content merely to give historical information or to entertain. Matthew wanted to convert his readers to a new way of thinking and living.[2] Specifically, Matthew's story explains why readers should accept the claim that Jesus is Israel's long-awaited Messiah and Son of God; it invites readers to become faithful followers of Jesus; it offers instructions on how to do so; and it provides both positive and negative examples of discipleship.

If Matthew's reason for writing was to assist in the church's mission of making disciples of all nations, then his intended audience was much broader than scholars sometimes imagine.[3] In contrast with most of Paul's letters, the Gospel of Matthew was not written for a single community that the author knew well. Instead, Matthew hoped his Gospel would circulate as widely as possible. A hint of that hope appears in Matthew 24:14, where Jesus predicts, "And this good news of the kingdom will be proclaimed throughout the world, as a testimony to all the nations; and then the end will come." Likewise, Jesus predicts in 26:13, "wherever this good news is proclaimed in the whole world, what she has done will be told in remembrance of her."

Based on the instructions in Matthew 10:5-15 and the example of missionaries like Paul, we can imagine a common setting for the reading of Matthew's story in the first century. Whenever Christian missionaries came to a new city, they looked for a worthy household, a household that would welcome them. First-century households typically included a patron (or head of the household) along with everyone else who came under the patron's control and protection. The presence of slaves, free workers, and the patron's extended family meant that households were often quite large. As a result, the worthy household provided an audience as well as hospitality. Missionaries told their hosts a story about the life, death, and resurrection of Jesus. That story led naturally to an invitation to become followers of Jesus through repentance and baptism. Anyone who accepted the invitation received further instruction in how to follow Jesus, including the expectation that they should learn the story and share it with others. Greco-Roman patrons expected to make religious decisions for their entire household, so a patron who was not converted might punish Christians within the household. On the other hand, converting the patron to Christianity usually meant that the entire household was converted. A house with a Christian patron could become the social center and the meeting place for a new congregation.

This style of evangelism did not necessarily require a written gospel. Christian missionaries had been telling the gospel for about a generation before anyone wrote it down. The need for a written gospel emerged as the earliest witnesses died and as the church continued to spread. Even then, however, writing did not take the place of oral storytelling. The gospels were written in Greek, which at the time had no paragraphs, punctuation, or spaces between words. Deciphering a Greek text was hard work even for experts. Few people could read, and those who could still preferred oral communication. Silent reading was very unusual. The main reason for writing a gospel was to ensure that it could be memorized and performed correctly.[4]

Students in ancient Greek schools were taught to recite stories dramatically and to get their audiences involved. Good stories included many opportunities for listeners to cheer the hero or hiss at the villain.[5] By that criterion, Matthew's story is a good one. Its hero is perfect, and its villains are evil. It is full of dramatic tension and suspense. Readers today may miss the drama, partly because the story is so familiar to us, but the situation was different for Matthew's intended audience. Matthew wrote for a world in which few people had heard of Jesus, and Matthew's concern for evangelism suggests that first-time listeners were very important to him. Their experience hearing the story could determine whether they returned for more training in discipleship. It is not surprising, then, that Matthew used suspense as a way of engaging first-time listeners emotionally. For example, Matthew 1:21 claims Jesus will save his people from their sins, but much of the story calls that promise into question. The suspense builds as more and more people reject Jesus and even his closest followers prove unfaithful. Readers must wonder how Jesus can possibly save these people from their sins. This use of suspense suggests that Matthew expected first-time listeners and others to hear the story from beginning to end in one sitting. A complete performance would have taken about three hours, but the time would have passed quickly.

If our conclusions about Matthew's intended audience are correct, then we rarely experience the story as it was meant to be read. When we hear short passages in worship or in Sunday school, we are not always reminded of the whole story. When we read silently alone, we miss hearing the story as part of a community of people being taught by Jesus. The audience of a passion play might come closer to the kind of experience Matthew hoped to evoke, but even they would miss the more intimate setting of a household.

Perhaps we will never have "the perfect gospel-reading experience," but with the Spirit's help we *can* listen to Matthew's story about Jesus with fresh ears. We can allow the story to touch us emotionally, spiritually, and intellectually. As we enter the story, we can find ourselves in the presence of the crucified but risen Jesus, who offers life in God's reign as a costly gift and who challenges us to embody that reign more fully in our life together. There is no substitute for reading the Gospel itself; but, as a preparation for that experience, it may be helpful to review briefly how the story flows from beginning to end.

The Flow of Matthew's Story

Like many well-told stories, Matthew's has three main parts: a beginning (1:1–4:16), a middle (4:17–16:20), and an end (16:21–28:20).[6] The first part introduces Jesus as the Son of God and the promised Messiah of Israel. Jesus' identity is revealed first through a royal genealogy and then through a series of events Matthew cites as the fulfillment of prophecy. Five times in the infancy narrative alone, Matthew introduces quotations with words like "This took place to fulfill what had been spoken by the Lord through the prophet" (1:22; 2:5, 15, 17, 23). Prophetic predictions show that the events of Jesus' life are not happenstance. God is at work. God sets the story in motion by causing Jesus to be born of Mary by the power of the Holy Spirit (1:18). God also announces through an angel that Jesus will "save his people from their sins" (1:21). As we have noted already, this announcement creates suspense by introducing the Messiah as a surprisingly vulnerable infant. How will he survive? What will happen to him? Early on we find out that God protects him from a divorce (1:19-24) and from murder (2:1-23), allowing him to grow up in exile. This presentation of

Jesus reaches a climax when a voice from heaven declares, "This is my Son, the Beloved, with whom I am well pleased" (3:17). Jesus' identity is further clarified as he rejects false expectations of the Son of God, choosing instead a life of humble service in complete obedience to God (4:1-11).

The theme of Jesus' identity continues throughout the rest of Matthew's story, but a new theme emerges in Matthew 4:17, marking the start of the second part: "From that time Jesus began to proclaim, 'Repent, for the kingdom of heaven has come near.' " The dominant theme in the second part of the story (4:17–16:20) is that Jesus proclaims the reign of heaven in both words and actions.

At the very beginning of this ministry Jesus calls disciples to share his work (4:18-22), and he instructs them in the greater righteousness that characterizes people who will enter the reign of heaven (5:1–7:27). Jesus preaches, teaches, and heals in such a way that he attracts huge crowds, who are amazed at his authority (4:23-25; 7:28-29; 8:1–9:34). In spite of Jesus' popularity, however, his mission in Galilee is rejected by both the religious leaders and the crowds. By forgiving sins and associating with sinners, Jesus sparks opposition from Israel's religious leaders, who are jealous of him and do not acknowledge his authority (9:2-13, 34). Jesus, in turn, charges that the religious leaders do not understand God's mercy (9:13). After sending the twelve disciples to minister on his behalf (9:35–10:42), Jesus determines that neither John the Baptist's ministry nor his own has moved the people to repent (11:16-19). Jesus, therefore, announces God's judgment against the cities of Galilee (11:20-24), even as he extends an open invitation for the people to come and receive true rest from him (11:25-30). After Jesus begins to fulfill that promise by healing on the sabbath (12:1-13), his conflict with the religious leaders becomes so intense they begin plotting to kill him (12:14).

Faced with rejection by both the religious leaders and the crowds, Jesus begins to teach in parables so the mysteries of the reign of heaven will be revealed only to the disciples (13:1-53). Jesus defends the disciples against accusations by the religious leaders (12:1-8; 15:1-20). He uses the disciples in feeding the crowds (14:13-21; 15:32-39), but privately he confronts them with their limited faith and understanding (14:31; 15:16; 16:8-9). Although the disciples do not always meet Jesus' expectations, they are at least able to grow in understanding. More importantly, God reveals to them that Jesus is the Messiah, the Son of the living God (14:22-33; cf. 8:27). When Peter confesses this truth on behalf of them all, Jesus responds with a promise to use Peter as the foundation of his church, an enduring community of disciples (16:13-20). The account of Peter's confession and blessing is the climax of the middle part of Matthew's story.

We have seen that Jesus' identity remains an important concern during the middle part of the story, even though the dominant theme is Jesus' proclamation of the reign of heaven. Something similar happens during the third part of the story. Like voices in a three-part fugue, the themes continue while a new one becomes prominent. The new theme is announced in 16:21: "From that time on, Jesus began to show his disciples that he must go to Jerusalem and undergo great suffering at the hands of the elders and chief priests and scribes, and be killed, and on the third day be raised." Although Jesus remains in Galilee until 19:1, the story's focus shifts in 16:21 to the fate that awaits Jesus in Jerusalem.

Two conflicts demand readers' attention throughout the third part of Matthew's story. First, Jesus' conflict with the religious leaders only intensifies as he confronts them in their seat of power. The second major conflict, between Jesus and his disciples, raises equally serious questions about how Jesus will complete his mission.

There are hints of this second conflict earlier in the story, but it explodes into the open immediately after Jesus begins to predict his suffering and death. Peter refuses to accept this prediction and rebukes Jesus privately (16:22). In response, Jesus calls Peter "Satan" and "a stumbling block," and he warns the disciples that they must all be ready for crucifixion (16:23-26). The spark that ignites this explosion is a basic disagreement over the role of Israel's Messiah. Jesus has determined that his role in God's reign is to serve others and to accept the suffering that comes as a result of that choice. The disciples expect the Messiah to be a triumphant ruler, and they hope to share his power over others. Since they misunderstand Jesus' role, they are not yet prepared to follow his example of service and suffering.

A related source of conflict is the disciples' chronic shortage of faith. In 17:14-20, Jesus accuses the disciples of being part of a "faithless and perverse generation," because they have failed to cure a child. Jesus has already authorized the disciples to perform this kind of healing

(10:8). Their failure suggests that they are not yet ready to continue Jesus' work after his death and resurrection. The disciples' conflict with Jesus is serious enough that he complains about having to be with them (17:17); nevertheless, they continue to travel toward Jerusalem together (17:22, 24; 19:1, 10). Immediately before (17:22-23), and then during the journey (20:17-19), Jesus repeats his prediction of suffering, death, and resurrection in Jerusalem. The disciples understand him well enough to be very upset (17:23), but the conflict remains unresolved.

This ongoing conflict between Jesus and his disciples helps explain the urgency of the warnings in Matthew 18. Jesus is not just giving the disciples advice about how to run the church; he is calling for a drastic change in the way they think and live. Jesus expects the disciples to continue his mission during the hard times that will follow his death and resurrection. Unfortunately, their arrogance and inadequate faith remain in the way. Only one month remains before the Passover,[7] and in that time Jesus must convince them to change from arrogant status-seekers to humble servants.

Matthew 18 is not the only speech in which Jesus seeks reconciliation with his disciples. Like Matthew 18, the speeches in 16:24-28 and 20:20-28 come after a prediction of Jesus' suffering, followed by a misguided question or comment from the disciples. In each case, Jesus renews his call for the disciples to follow his example of humble, suffering service. Matthew does not mention the disciples' response to any of these speeches, but their need for repeated correction implies that the message is not getting through. For example, the disciples turn away children soon after Jesus has said to welcome them (18:5; 19:13), and the disciples continue to vie for places of honor after Jesus has taught them that humble people are the greatest in God's eyes (18:1-4; 20:20-28).

Both of the story's major conflicts, conflict with the authorities and conflict with the disciples, reach a climax during the Passover celebration in Jerusalem. On entering the city, Jesus confronts the religious leaders in the temple (21:12-17) and engages them in a heated debate (21:23–22:46). After announcing and lamenting God's judgment against them (23:1-39), Jesus leaves the temple and teaches the disciples privately about God's end-time judgment (24:1–25:46). Since the religious leaders are unable to shame Jesus in a public debate, they conspire to arrest him secretly (26:3-5), receiving unexpected help from a disciple (26:14-16, 47-49). In keeping with God's will (26:39, 42, 52-54) and in order to establish a covenant of forgiveness for many people (20:28; 26:28), Jesus allows himself to be arrested, tried, and crucified (27:15-44). Although the religious leaders cannot find reliable testimony against Jesus, the high priests convict him for refusing to deny he is the Son of God (26:59-68). Pilate, the Roman governor, pleases the crowds and religious leaders by sentencing Jesus to death in spite of his innocence (27:1-2, 11-26). Jesus is mocked by the religious leaders and others who view his execution as proof that he is not the Messiah (27:38-44). At Jesus' death, however, he is attested as the Son of God through supernatural portents and through the confession they draw from a centurion (27:51-54). On the third day after the crucifixion, God vindicates and exalts Jesus by raising him from the dead. The religious leaders use lies and bribery to cover up the resurrection (28:11-15), but their continued opposition is futile in light of God's decisive action. God has given "all authority in heaven and on earth" to Jesus (28:18).

The disciples' conflict with Jesus also reaches its terrible climax on Passover night, when they deliver, desert, and deny him. Jesus has repeatedly predicted that he will be "delivered" into the hands of his enemies, the religious leaders. During the Passover meal, he reveals the shocking news that one of the disciples will be the "deliverer" (26:20-25). After the meal, the dire predictions keep coming: All the disciples will desert Jesus, and Peter will three times deny knowing him (26:30-35). The disciples' refusal to believe these predictions shows they remain arrogant and deluded (26:22, 33-35). Events unfold as Jesus has predicted, leaving the disciples (represented by Peter) weeping with remorse (26:75). Peter's tears are a sign he and the others are finally ready to repent.

The resurrection is a God-given opportunity for the scattered disciples to be gathered and reconciled with Jesus. He appears first to the loyal women, and he sends them to gather the eleven so they can meet him in Galilee as predicted (26:32; 28:9-10). It is no coincidence that Jesus' last act before leaving Galilee was to teach the disciples about confronting and forgiving a brother who has sinned (18:15-35). By calling the eleven "my brothers" and summoning them back to Galilee, Jesus shows he has forgiven them (28:10). In a final, climactic scene, Jesus is reunited with the disciples, who worship him in spite of their continued doubts. Jesus then commands them to make disciples of all nations, reversing his earlier limitations on their mission and repeating his promise to be with them always (28:19-20). Matthew's final scene resolves the suspense about how Jesus will fulfill his mission of saving his people from their sins. Although readers already know that Jesus' death and resurrection have established a new covenant of forgiveness for all who will accept it, the final scene shows how the news of that covenant will spread. Jesus will work through his followers, empowering them to baptize and teach new disciples from every nation. Jesus' followers are still not perfect, but they are finally ready for their job.

Now would be a good time to set this book aside and pick up the Gospel of Matthew. Read the Gospel out loud from beginning to end with as much feeling as you can muster. If you can find an audience, so much the better. Then return here for some additional reflections about the good news we have found in Matthew's story.

Finding Grace in the Story

One way to enter a story emotionally is to empathize with one or more of the characters. Since Matthew's original purpose was to "make disciples," it comes as no surprise that many aspects of the story encourage readers to identify with the twelve disciples. For example, readers get to listen in on teachings the disciples receive privately from Jesus. Two of these teaching sessions, including Matthew 18, take place in a house (13:1, 36; 17:25), which is like the setting where Matthew expected his story to be recited. In such a setting, it would be easy for the audience to imagine they were among the circle of disciples being taught by Jesus. His promises, blessings, and warnings for the disciples are worded so they apply to readers as well.

Readers who identify with the disciples soon find themselves caught in Matthew's evangelistic fishing net. The disciples start out well on their journey with Jesus, giving up everything to follow him. As the story continues, however, they fail miserably, leaving readers to decide whether they themselves could do any better under the circumstances. Matthew asks, in effect, "Do you have the faith to walk on water? cast out a demon? be arrested and crucified with Jesus?" If readers imagine they can do better than the ones who deserted Jesus, then they are thinking like Peter in the garden: "Though all become deserters because of you, I will never desert you" (26:33). The end of the story leaves readers little choice but to conclude that such thinking is a delusion. Instead, readers who identify fully with the disciples are led toward a more honest confession: "We are at least as fallible and sinful as the disciples in the story who deserted Jesus. Just as they desperately needed to be forgiven and restored, so do we." Such a confession breaks down pride and self-sufficiency, freeing readers to be reconciled with the One who loves them in spite of their failures. Like the eleven disciples at the end of the story, readers can come into the presence of the risen Jesus, restored through grace and ready to share that grace with others. Readers can be different from Judas, whose remorse is genuine but whose suicide prevents him from receiving forgiveness within the story.

Of course, Matthew's story includes characters that are better examples than the twelve disciples named in 10:2-4. Some of the best examples of faith are characters who appear for only one scene, such as a centurion (8:5-13), the friends of a paralytic (9:2-8), a woman with a hemorrhage (9:20-22), and a Canaanite woman (15:21-28). In Matthew 27:55, readers learn that many women also followed Jesus from Galilee and helped support him financially. These women do not desert Jesus in the end, and two of them are the first witnesses of his resurrection. It is not surprising then that some readers identify with these exemplary minor characters more easily than with the Twelve.[8]

Such readers can also find grace in the story, though perhaps in a different form. Matthew's miracle accounts sometimes emphasize forgiveness as well as physical healing (9:2-8), but forgiveness is not always the most needed form of grace. Other forms include compassion for those who are suffering, freedom for the oppressed, hope and affirmation for those who are usually rejected or ignored. When Jesus accepts support from the women who have followed him, he is both giving and receiving grace. A mutually supportive relationship with Jesus is also available to readers.

Of course, Matthew's most exemplary character is Jesus, the hero of the story. It is difficult for ordinary readers to identify with some of the traits Matthew ascribes to Jesus (for example, power over nature and knowledge of the future). To some extent, however, many readers can identify with Jesus' experience of unjust suffering. Whether or not we have been persecuted for our faith, we will eventually experience the hard truth that God does not always protect God's children from harm. At such times, the cry, "My God, my God, why have you forsaken me!" may ring true (27:46). For readers who identify with Jesus on the cross, Matthew's story offers grace in the form of hope. God never really forsakes us, not even in death. Just as God used Jesus' suffering for a mighty purpose, God can bring good out of the tragedies we experience. We, like Jesus, will be raised from the dead.

We have seen that Matthew's story offers grace in various forms to readers who identify with Jesus, the disciples, or other exemplary characters. Is there also grace for readers who identify with the religious leaders? This question is difficult because Matthew's view of the religious leaders is so negative. The story portrays them all as merciless, murdering hypocrites; and tragically that stereotype has contributed to the negative stereotyping of Jews for centuries. Recently, historians have drawn on various sources to give a more balanced picture of the Jewish leadership in Jesus' time. For example, the Pharisees had a deep concern for the religious life of the common people.[9] On the whole, they were probably at least as sincere as the leaders of Christian congregations and other religious institutions today.

Since virtually all the characters in Matthew's story (including Jesus) are Jewish, it does not make sense to identify the religious leaders in the story with "the Jews." In fact, Christians who make that identification may be letting themselves off the hook (or out of the net) too easily. A wiser and humbler approach would be to ask whether we are in any way like Matthew's portrait of the religious leaders. Do our actions measure up to our words? Is our righteousness mainly an outward appearance, or does it reach the very center of our lives, producing right relationships with God and other people? Are we ever jealous of other people's authority? Do we sometimes focus on minor rules while neglecting "the weightier matters of the law: justice and mercy and faith" (23:23)? Matthew encourages this type of self-critique by warning readers not to become like the religious leaders in the story (23:1-12).

If readers identify with the religious leaders enough to repent and seek forgiveness, then Matthew's story is doing its job once again. Certainly, there are harsh words against the religious leaders, including accusations that they are responsible for the death of Jesus; nevertheless, Matthew also shows that they can be forgiven. Jesus expresses his willingness to forgive most clearly in Matthew 26:28: "for this is my blood of the covenant, which is poured out for many for the forgiveness of sins." At other points in the story, blood is a symbol of guilt (23:35; 27:4, 24-29), but Jesus' words at Passover give his blood a new meaning.[10] Jesus intends for his blood to be a sign of the forgiveness he offers "for many," meaning "for all who accept it." Thus, Matthew's story offers grace in the form of forgiveness to all readers, including those who identify with the religious leaders.

The title of this chapter suggests that Matthew's story is "about Jesus." Certainly that is true, but we have also seen that his story is about God's grace. Not every character in the story accepts the grace God offers through Jesus, but the offer still extends to every character and every reader. As we study challenging passages like Matthew 18, we need to remember that they appear in the context of a story about grace. Otherwise, our discipleship can become a dreary discipline instead of a joyful privilege rooted in thanksgiving.

Our Stories

We have seen that Matthew's story offers grace to its readers; nevertheless, an offer remains just an offer until it is accepted, and Matthew's story is only a story until readers enter into a living relationship with the hero. As Christians, we confess that Jesus is much more than a character in a story or a great figure from the past. Jesus is alive, the Lord of all creation and the merciful Savior of all who trust him. Jesus seeks to build a loving, trusting relationship with every person on earth. People who accept that relationship also receive life in God's reign, the only life that ultimately matters.

Both of this book's authors have come to know Jesus personally as Savior and Lord, and we have experienced God's grace in that relationship. Our stories may not be unusual or remarkable, nor do we present them as examples for others to follow. We share them, however, as part of our testimony that the grace Matthew wrote about is real. Here is part of Dan's story:

I grew up in a Christian home where church attendance and family devotions were a normal part of life. Unless I was running a fever, I went to church, and usually I didn't mind. We went to the Bridgewater Church of the Brethren, a large congregation near a church-related college, where the standards for preaching, music, and children's programming were rather high. Robert L. Sherfy was pastor during most of my growing-up years, and I remember with gratitude the way he made sermons interesting for children. Most sermons stressed what we could do for Jesus, rather than what Jesus had done for us. By the time Pastor Sherfy baptized me at age twelve, I understood that I was making a lifelong commitment, turning my back on sin and giving my whole self to God.

Perhaps I sinned more than I remember, but what I remember most is working hard to comply with the expectations of my parents and other authority figures, including God. If I resisted my parents or teachers, I did so passively. My conscience echoed my parents' values, but with an added note of sternness. Two of my chief sins were pride and perfectionism, but I didn't realize at the time how sinful they were or how they kept me from accepting a deeper and more joyful relationship with God.

Fortunately, my understanding of God's grace has grown along with the awareness that I need grace. It has been a slow, uneven process that continues to this day. Instead of being converted in one dramatic moment like Paul, I identify with Peter's experience of multiple conversions. Little by little, I am learning to rely more on God and less on myself, to accept God's acceptance of me, and to focus on loving people instead of making an impression.

One experience that helped me grow in grace took place while I was an exchange student for a year in Barcelona, Spain. I had planned to visit and study a variety of Spanish churches, but instead I became very involved in the first congregation I visited. It was appropriately called the *Iglesia Bautista de Gracia* (Grace Baptist Church). Protestants are a small minority in Spain, and at that time memories of persecution under the late dictator Franco were quite fresh. That congregation had experienced the cost of discipleship in a way I had not, but what I learned most from them that year was to "rejoice in the Lord." The congregation and especially the youth could hardly stop singing and clapping. The source of their joy was God's grace. They knew what God had done for them, and they were ready to say so to anyone who would listen. During a year of singing and praying with them, the message of God's grace began to seep from my head down to my heart. I prayed eagerly and often because I felt God's presence and love so strongly. Those were the prayers in which I first heard God calling me to ministry.

God's grace came to Jan in a way that changed her life dramatically:

Following a particularly violent, abusive argument with my mother, I was depressed and hopeless. A lifetime of futilely seeking to please my mother and to earn and deserve her love had brought me to this point. I prayed a prayer of wretched surrender as I fell into a tearful sleep. God said, "I have opened your heart and I have filled it with my love and my grace." This glorious message was spoken to me in a dream nearly ten years ago. God answered my desperate prayer. Love and grace are not earned or deserved. They are given.

God's grace-filled message was a jolting, wake-up call. It ignited a marvelous rebirth of my spiritual journey. My journey has taken me through seminary, a call to ministry, and to my first pastorate. Grace, exemplified by the life, death and resurrection of Jesus, continues to be my teacher. I identify with Paul's dramatic conversion. My dream was my Damascus Road experience. I identify with Peter's plodding, repeated discoveries. I continue to forget and relearn how grace is present and active in my life. I identify with the great faith of the women who knew Jesus, the Canaanite woman and the woman who anointed Jesus. My journey into grace is a daily adventure that brings countless opportunities to receive and give grace. There is no limit.

God's grace is real! Even as we testify to our experiences of grace, we invite you to remember and share your own experiences. How has

God reached you with love, compassion, healing, or forgiveness? If you yearn for a deeper experience of God's grace, your yearning is evidence that God is already at work within your heart and mind. You can open yourself further to God's work by being completely honest with God and by saying yes to the good news of Jesus' forgiveness.

The appropriate response to God's grace is obedient discipleship, but grace must come first. When we lose sight of God's grace, our attempts to practice discipleship according to Matthew 18 tend to be dreary at best and oppressive at worst. The more we remember God's grace, the more discipleship becomes a joy and a privilege.

Questions for Discussion

1. This chapter presents one way of understanding the author, purpose, and intended audience of Matthew's story. How does that historical background enhance your understanding of Matthew 18?

2. How would you describe Matthew's "audience" today? You may want to focus on your church or your group or Sunday school class within the church.

3. The authors suggest that the Gospel of Matthew was designed to be read aloud from beginning to end. Reflect on the differences between that way of experiencing the Gospel and ways that are more common today, such as silent reading or the reading of brief passages. Did you accept the challenge to read the entire Gospel of Matthew aloud? If so, what insights did you gain from that experience?

4. The authors suggest that Matthew 18 should be interpreted in light of a sharp, ongoing conflict between Jesus and his disciples. What, if any, "conflict" do you have with Jesus or Jesus' teachings?

5. How do you relate to the examples of grace in Matthew's story? Are you able to identify with the disciples, the people who come for healing, Jesus, the religious leaders, or other figures in the story? With whom do you identify most? Why?

6. Do you have a testimony of grace? Please share it.

NOTES

1. For various perspectives regarding the author, see Richard B. Gardner, *Matthew*, Believers Church Bible Commentary (Scottdale, Pa.: Herald Press, 1991), 20-22; and Craig S. Keener, *A Commentary on the Gospel of Matthew* (Grand Rapids: Eerdmans, 1999), 38-41.

2. David E. Aune, *The New Testament in Its Literary Environment* (Philadelphia: The Westminster Press, 1987), 46-76, provides a helpful comparison between the Gospels and other ancient biographies.

3. William G. Thompson is one of many scholars who assume that the Gospel of Matthew's intended audience was small and well known to the author. That assumption weakens Thompson's otherwise excellent study of Matthew 18 entitled *Matthew's Advice to a Divided Community, Mt. 17, 22–18, 35* (Rome: Biblical Institute Press, 1970).

4. Paul J. Achtemeier, *"Omne verbum sonat*: The New Testament and the Oral Environment of Late Western Antiquity," *Journal of Biblical Literature*, 1990, 3-27.

5. Whitney Shiner, "Disciples and Death: Audience Reaction to Mark 8:27–9:1 and 10:35-45" (Unpublished paper presented at the 2000 Annual Meeting of Society of Biblical Literature, Nashville, Tenn., November 18, 2000).

6. Jack Dean Kingsbury, *Matthew as Story*, 2nd ed. (Philadelphia: Fortress Press, 1988), 40. The following summary also draws heavily on Kingsbury's work.

7. The tax mentioned in Matthew 17:24-27 was collected from all free Jewish men during the month before Passover.

8. See, for example, Janice Capel Anderson, "Gender and Reading," *Semeia*, 1984, 71-89.

9. For a widely accepted history of the Pharisees, see Jacob Neusner, *From Politics to Piety: The Emergence of Pharisaic Judaism* (Englewood Cliffs, N.J.: Prentice Hall, 1973).

10. Timothy B. Cargal, " 'His Blood Be Upon Us and Upon Our Children': A Matthean Double Entendre?" *New Testament Studies* 37 (1991): 101-12.

3

Great Humility
Matthew 18:1-4

¹At that time the disciples came to Jesus and asked, "Who is the greatest in the kingdom of heaven?" ² He called a child, whom he put among them, ³ and said, "Truly I tell you, unless you change and become like children, you will never enter the kingdom of heaven. ⁴ Whoever becomes humble like this child is the greatest in the kingdom of heaven."

The Biblical Story

In the last chapter, we observed that Jesus is in sharp conflict with his disciples during the third part of Matthew's story (16:21–28:20) and that Matthew 18 is one of several speeches in which Jesus seeks to overcome that conflict. Jesus is counting on the disciples to continue his mission after his death and resurrection, but the disciples are not prepared to serve others as Jesus does. They lack the necessary faith, and they are too focused on gaining a high status for themselves. Remembering this narrative context will be important as we begin a more detailed study of Matthew 18. We will see that Jesus wastes no time in confronting the disciples' arrogance.

The first four verses are a key part of Matthew 18 because they state the overall theme of the speech, namely, that humble people are greatest in the reign of heaven. The longer teaching sections in Matthew are typically organized around a theme related to the reign of heaven,[1] and Matthew 18 appears to fit that pattern. Matthew 18:1-4 states the theme outright in Jesus' answer to the disciples' initial question. The disciples ask, "Who is greatest in the kingdom of heaven?" and the answer is, "Whoever becomes humble like this child is the greatest in the kingdom of heaven." The conversation could easily end at this point. When Jesus continues to speak without further prompting, he seems to be elaborating on the answer that he has just given. The importance of verses 1-4 will become even clearer as we compare Matthew 18 with the Sermon on the Mount. Both speeches begin with a comment that the disciples approached Jesus (5:1; 18:1),[2] and both end with the words "When Jesus had finished saying these things . . ." (7:28; 19:1). More importantly, both speeches elaborate on themes that are stated using similar words:

	SERMON ON THE MOUNT	MATTHEW 18
Thematic Statements (with shared words in italics)	"*Whoever* breaks one of the least of these commandments, and teaches others to do the same, will be called least in the kingdom of heaven; but *whoever* does them and teaches them will be called *great in the kingdom of heaven.* For *I tell you, unless* your righteousness exceeds that of the scribes and Pharisees, *you will never enter the kingdom of heaven*" (5:19-20).	"Truly *I tell you, unless* you change and become like children, *you will never enter the kingdom of heaven. Whoever* becomes humble like this child is the *greatest in the kingdom of heaven*" (18:3-4).

The rest of the Sermon on the Mount describes the kind of righteousness the disciples will need in order to enter the reign of heaven (or kingdom of heaven, as it is translated in the NRSV). Likewise, each of the values emphasized in Matthew 18:5-35 relates in some way to the idea that humble people are greatest in God's reign.[3]

Matthew 18 has often been interpreted as a speech about relationships within the church, but the thematic statement in 18:1-4 does not refer to "the church," but to "the [reign] of heaven." In order to clarify the theme, we need to ask what Matthew means by these two important terms. "The [reign] of heaven" has the same meaning as "the [reign] of God" in other Gospels.[4] It is Matthew's "primary metaphor for God's saving activity."[5] *Reign* is a better translation than "kingdom," because it refers to the act of ruling more than to a territory or a group of people as kingdom does. To enter the reign of heaven is to participate in God's saving activity and thus to enter life. Meanwhile, "the church" in Matthew's story refers to the community of disciples Jesus has already begun to build, starting with the call of Peter and Andrew (4:18-22; 16:18).[6] Matthew's story associates the reign of heaven with the church but never equates them. The disciples as a community are called to live within God's reign, but whether they will do so remains an open question as the story unfolds. In Matthew 18:1, the disciples are probably thinking about themselves when they ask, "Who is greatest in the [reign] of heaven?" but they are being presumptuous, and Jesus corrects them (18:3).

The scene just before Matthew 18 helps explain why they are thinking about their own greatness (see 17:24-27). Soon after Jesus and the disciples enter Peter's hometown of Capernaum, some officials approach Peter to ask whether Jesus pays the "two drachmas," an annual tax collected from all free Jewish men to support the temple and its leadership. The tax, based on Exodus 30:11-16, was understood as a means of atonement, a kind of ransom that would restore one's relationship with God. Peter satisfies the officials by quickly answering yes; but Jesus is not satisfied and corrects Peter later by means of a parable and a miracle. Both the parable and the miracle are lessons in God's grace. The parable asks whether children of God are obliged to pay a tax for God's house. Earthly rulers do not tax their own families, and neither does God, who reigns in heaven. Therefore, Jesus pays the temple tax not out of obligation, but out of love. In this case, he graciously pays in order not to give offense to the religious leaders. Jesus next tells Peter to find money for the tax in the mouth of the first fish he catches. This miracle is ideally suited for Peter, who is used to earning his way through the hard work of fishing. Jesus playfully reminds Peter that he can depend on God to supply his needs, including his need for atonement.

The other disciples evidently hear the conversation between Jesus and Peter (or at least hear *about* it), because they want Jesus to clarify what he has just said. Unfortunately, this connection is lost in the NRSV, which fails to translate a Greek word meaning "so," "then," or "consequently." The disciples ask, "Who *then* is greatest in the [reign] of heaven?" probably because they are impressed with the privileges Peter has just been promised as a member of God's royal family. Readers might imagine that the disciples are becoming jealous at this point; Peter, however, usually acts as a representative of the Twelve, and there have been no previous hints of jealousy between them.[7] Another possibility is that the disciples feel encouraged by Jesus' conversation with Peter. They assume that God's reign is like earthly kingdoms in which people at the top have special privileges and power. If Peter, their representative, is a privileged member of God's family, then they cannot be far behind. Who knows? Maybe one of them will turn out to be even greater than Peter! Whether the other disciples are jealous of Peter or proud of him, their question shows how little they understand about the reign of heaven.

If the disciples are thinking about their own greatness, it makes sense that Jesus would sharply confront them in 18:2-4. He begins by placing a child in their midst as a visual parable of what it means to be great in God's eyes. In order to get Jesus' point, we need to imagine a small child standing in a circle of status-seeking grownups. The child is dwarfed both physically and socially.

Like the disciples, many of Matthew's original readers would have been used to looking down on children. Both Jewish and Gentile households typically had a clear pecking order, from the patron at the top, down through all his subordinates, with children and slaves at the bottom. Of course, many children were born into slavery, even free-born children were rarely the center of a family's attention. Paul was not exaggerating (at least not much) when he wrote in Galatians 4:1 that "heirs, as long as they are minors, are no better than slaves." Children, whether slave or free, had no rights and could be punished very severely. In most families they toiled alongside adults from sunrise to sunset beginning as early as age five. They were valued for their labor and for the security they could eventually provide their parents.[8]

Since the temple tax did not apply to children and slaves, Jesus' decision to call a child may also be related to his earlier conversation with Peter. The child is a reminder for the disciples that their divine tax exemption is not necessarily a mark of special privilege. In fact, it is just the opposite. Instead of being great in the sense of having power over others, the disciples are to be like children in God's household. They are dependent on God's grace, just as children are normally dependent on adults.[9]

The meaning of the visual parable becomes even sharper as Jesus interprets it in words: "Truly I tell you, unless you change and become like children, you will never enter the reign of heaven" (18:3). The Greek word translated "change" literally means "turn," but it can also mean "repent." Here Jesus demands nothing less than a complete change of heart as a condition for entering the reign of heaven. In other words, the disciples should stop imagining that they are great in the reign of heaven and concentrate instead on getting in.

The next sentence answers the disciples' question directly and further explains what it means for the disciples to "become like children." For Matthew, children serve as an example of humility. The point is not that children naturally have a humble attitude, nor that the child summoned by Jesus is especially humble. The word translated "become humble" in 18:4 literally means "lower oneself," and it has to do with a change in social status. In other words, Jesus is telling the disciples to seek the low status of children. If they want to be great in God's eyes, they need to climb down the social ladder, not up. In a later speech, Jesus repeats the same idea, using slavery as the illustration of humility instead of childhood: "Whoever wishes to be great among you must be your servant, and whoever wishes to be first among you must be your slave" (20:26-27).

It is important to note that Jesus directs this message to free adult men who are used to having at least some power over others. The disciples in Matthew's story may not be wealthy, but neither are they the poorest of the poor. Four of them had boats and nets, and one had a tax office before leaving to follow Jesus (4:18-22; 9:9). Peter evidently remains a homeowner and head of a household even after his call (8:14). There is still room for the disciples to seek a lower social status, and Jesus calls them to do so voluntarily, as part of their decision to seek

God's reign above all else. In order to make this change, the disciples will need a humble attitude. Jesus does not insist that people who are already low (like the child) must stay where they are, but neither does he urge them to climb the existing social ladder. Instead, he announces God's decision to give the greatest honor and blessing to those who are at the bottom, a decision that makes the ladder itself obsolete.[10]

Throughout Matthew's story, the example of Jesus' life helps to reinforce the ladder-leveling message that the least are really the greatest in God's reign. Soon after the announcement of Jesus' birth in 1:25, the story features a contest between two very different kings. Since Herod was officially named "king of the Jews" by decree of the Roman Senate in 40 B.C., irony abounds when the magi enter Jerusalem inquiring, "Where is the child who has been born king of the Jews?" (2:2). As the rightful heir to the throne of David, Jesus has a legitimate claim to that title (1:1-17). Instead he is simply called "the child" (2:2, 8, 9, 11, 13, 14, 20, 21). Herod is both hypocritical and ruthless in attempting to eliminate his potential rival. In spite of his great earthly power, however, he cannot thwart God's plans. Jesus survives the massacre at Bethlehem, and Herod promptly dies (2:19). Herod, who considers himself great, turns out to be powerless, especially powerless over death; the one who is truly great is the child backed by God.[11]

As the story continues, Jesus demonstrates "great humility" in his ministry, death, and resurrection. Jesus acts with authority from God, but he uses that authority for the benefit of others in humble ways. Jesus is "gentle and humble in heart," so he gives rest to those who accept the easy yoke of his teaching (11:29). As a healer, he fulfills Isaiah's prophecy concerning the suffering servant of God (Isa. 42:1-4; 53:4; Matt. 8:16-17; 12:15-21). He does not draw attention to himself, but quietly serves the people who come to him for help. When Jesus enters Jerusalem, he comes as a "gentle" king, not a conqueror. The ultimate demonstration of Jesus' humility is that he gives his life for others in obedience to God's will. Although tempted to come down from the cross (27:40), he willingly gives up his spirit as an act of obedience (27:50). Finally, the resurrection begins to fulfill Jesus' prediction that the "meek will inherit the earth" (5:5; 28:18).

Matthew's story repeatedly emphasizes Jesus' greatness as well as his humility (11:11; 12:39-42; 22:41-45); therefore, we can surmise how Matthew would answer the disciples' question in 18:1. *Jesus* is the greatest in the reign of heaven! It would not be appropriate for Jesus to declare his own greatness in this passage, but the truth comes across anyway because of the way in which Matthew links Jesus with the child. We have already noted that Matthew 1–2 repeatedly refers to Jesus as "the child." Matthew 18:5 makes the connection even more explicit: "Whoever welcomes one such child in my name welcomes me." Finally, Jesus promises the disciples that he will be "among them" (18:20), even as the child is "among them" (18:2). In Matthew's story, Jesus is the prime example of both childlike humility and true greatness. Jesus could demand high honors as the Son of God and as Israel's long-promised Messiah, but he chooses instead to take the lowly roles of a child and slave.

When Jesus tells the disciples to repent and become like children, he is inviting them to share his kind of greatness, and the invitation is open to anyone. Greatness in God's eyes consists in humble service instead of privilege, in going down the social ladder instead of up. The opportunities for "advancement" are endless.

Our Stories

Finding stories about contemporary Christians who are trying to practice humility can be difficult. Humble people tend not to brag about themselves and may go unnoticed by others. Fortunately, humility is closely connected with service in Matthew's vocabulary, and it seems easier for people to speak about serving others.

This story, which is well known in the Church of the Brethren, illustrates both humility and service. On the last day of business at the 1948 Annual Conference, a young woman by the name of Alma Moyers had an unusual request for that year's moderator, Dr. Calvert N. Ellis. The young adults attending the conference wanted to propose that the church establish an ongoing program of volunteer service. The conference had been full of inspiring messages about the suffering that continued after World War II, and the young adults had gathered for daily prayer vigils, seeking guidance about how to respond. The group had circulated a survey asking who would be willing to give a year of their lives in service without pay; eighty-nine percent had said yes. There was enormous energy to begin right away, but they had not followed proper procedures for getting an item on the Annual Conference agenda. These procedures normally take a year or more to process and involve debates at the congregational, district, and national levels. Alma Moyers Long recalls her meeting with Moderator Ellis in these words:

> It was just before the afternoon session. I was back behind this curtain, and I had this paper in my hand. I felt like a mouse against a giant. I told him the young people have an idea they'd like to bring up at Conference. I felt like I was only two inches high. . . .
>
> He said, "Well, we've never done this before. Standing Committee has to pass on everything."
>
> Of course, I knew that. Dan West had already told us he didn't know if we could get this done. Calvert Ellis didn't put us down. He just said, "We'll see what we can do about it."[12]

As a college president, Calvert Ellis was not inflexible, but he understood the need to consider new programs carefully. As he admitted later, he was not convinced that the young adults' proposal would amount to anything; nevertheless, after consulting with the other officers at the podium, he agreed to "listen to the young people." The delegates voted to reopen the agenda, and Ted Chambers came as the group's representative to present their motion. Ted was only 4 feet 10 inches tall. He needed an orange crate in order to reach the microphone. "Ladies and gentlemen," he began, "I'm Ted Chambers from Grand Rapids, Michigan, and, believe it or not, I'm twenty-two years old."[13] People laughed, and Ted followed that ice-breaker with a very persuasive speech. The proposal passed by a large majority. Alma Moyers Long recalls, "When the young people stood up and cheered, the whole Conference was surprised. . . . It was just like Pentecost! Just like a football game! You could just feel the power of God in that place!"[14]

Since the 1948 Annual Conference, more than six thousand volunteers have served in Brethren Volunteer Service (BVS), which later became a model for the United States Peace Corps. BVS remains an extremely valuable program not only for the work the volunteers do, but also for what they learn in the process.[15] Many Brethren volunteers have gone on to become servant leaders in the church and in the world.

Tom Benevento was a Brethren Volunteer Service worker who learned a great deal from his experiences working in Guatemala with Trees for Life. His stories show deep respect for the poor of Guatemala, whose generosity often surprised him. Tom says that the following experience had a profound and humbling effect on him:

It was one of those difficult, crummy kind of days when I had to do errands in Guatemala City. It's a place I don't often look forward to going to, because of the heavy pollution, noise, crime, and crowdedness. That day was particularly dreary. . . . Along the edge of the street, with the noise of broken-mufflered cars, trucks, and buses, was a trail of garbage, plastic, and odd rotting smells. I tried only to focus on my feet that were protected by a favored pair of brown hiking boots. As I watched them touch the hard gray pavement, I was comforted by the thought of long hikes in the Highlands.

As I looked up when I reached the street corner, I noticed the light was green to cross over to the next block. Looking to my left and right, I saw vehicles moving in a maze of angles and directions. Amidst the noise and confusion, I noticed a man in the middle of the street on his hands and knees, crawling down the yellow double-lined center strip. Because of the confusion and the crossing of cars, I saw him for only a brief flash. The image of him hardly caught my attention as I reached the other side of the street corner.

Not until I carried myself down the next block had it registered in my mind what I had seen. This disabled man with deformed legs, dirty and crawling without shoes, nearly being hit by the high pace of cars, was probably one of the most on-the-edge human beings I had seen.

My . . . [feet] kept heading for the next block, but my mind had already turned around to follow him. Should I keep going? What could I do anyway? It would feel stupid to try and talk to him. After a couple of blocks, I finally resolved . . . to at least inform him of a hospital in Antigua called *Obras de Hermano Pedro* (Works of Brother Peter) that does high quality care for the disabled.

I turned around and caught up to him as he was making his way, crawling as he did, up the sidewalk. I squatted down to meet him at eye level. He had a gray stubby beard and an over-sized baseball cap pulled down in line with his eyebrows. His nose appeared to have been broken badly. I asked his name. "Juan," he replied, and started some small talk. I felt a little awkward and didn't know exactly what to say. I proceeded to explain about the hospital in Antigua. To my surprise, he said he knew the place. In fact, he lived there for eleven years. . . . In amazement, I watched his face and listened to him. He said, "I've decided to leave the hospital and come back to the city, because I wanted to take care of my mother. She is nearly ninety years old, you know."

I realized that Juan makes his way out into the streets each day, moving across the cold pavement, dodging the traffic, to request pocket change of by-passers to help with the upkeep and food at home for his mother.

This wasn't supposed to be what happened. He was trying to take care of someone else. Things seemed flipped upside down. Here was a man that appeared helpless, but somehow he was trying to flip it the other way. At a distance, I could see Juan's marginalizing, dirty, and dehumanized state. . . . Yet at the same time, with a closer encounter I saw that he upheld, in an odd way, a kind of beauty and graced humanity at its best.[16]

Like Jesus himself and like the child in Matthew 18:1-4, Juan illustrates the paradox that the lowliest people are actually greatest in God's eyes. Tom's decisions model humility also. He could have earned good money in the United States, but he chose to serve for a while with no salary—and not only to serve but also to stop, listen, and learn.

Humble service comes in many forms. Robert Bowman served as pastor of the Easton (Maryland) Church of the Brethren from 1960 to 1964. Bob and his wife, Martha, are remembered very fondly there because of the way they nurtured the whole congregation, but they are quick to point out that the care was mutual. At a celebration for the fiftieth anniversary of the congregation's building, Bob shared this memory:

We had only lived in the parsonage for a few days when we were surprised to see a strange man in the front yard. He seemed to be looking very closely at one of the trees. So I went out, introduced myself, and asked, "Can I help you?" Well, it turned out that he was the one helping me. Jacob Geib had come by to pick the bag worms off the trees.

The anniversary crowd chuckled with delight, needing no further explanation. Jacob Geib was a long-time member of the congregation who had since passed away, but he was still famous for helping neighbors all over town with their gardening. Bob Bowman and Jacob Geib both proclaimed the gospel in Easton. Bob did it mostly with eloquent words; Jacob did it with willing hands.

Humble service toward others occurs daily in families. A couple is particularly blessed when their service is willing and mutual, rather than forced or one-sided. Norman L. Harsh shared this story about a couple that discovered a faithful way to symbolize their ideal of mutual service:

> It took two Ethiopian students at Virginia Tech University to put a new "spin" on the traditional Brethren expression of humility, feetwashing. In their home country, they were members of Orthodox and Sudan Interior Mission churches. During their stay at Blacksburg, Virginia, they became participants in the Good Shepherd Church of the Brethren, where I was pastor. In due time they asked me to officiate at their wedding.
>
> "But there's just one thing," the groom requested as the planning began. "We'd like to wash each other's feet as part of our ceremony."
>
> While doing serious Bible study in preparation for marriage, they discovered that feetwashing could be a satisfying expression of Paul's teaching about mutual submission (Eph. 5:21-33). It is a connection that long-time Brethren have ordinarily missed, but it has powerful implications for happiness in marriage. The couple carried out their insight at the wedding. In the process they gave a beautiful gift to their new-found sisters and brothers in Christ.[17]

Mutual submission in marriage was a radical idea in the first-century culture shared by Paul and Matthew. That culture taught men to rule over their wives, not submit to them. Even today, mutual submission is a difficult ideal to practice fairly. Many women have full-time jobs, but still carry the lion's share of responsibility for serving at home. It is women, far more often than men, who sacrifice their careers for the sake of marriage or parenting. Homemakers, whether men or women, may feel that their role is not valued.

The answer to this problem is not to reject the biblical ideal of mutual submission in marriage, but to seek more equality in the way it is practiced. Instead of reinforcing either traditional gender roles or newer social expectations, Matthew's teaching on humility can free both women and men to serve God in whatever way God calls. Socially prescribed norms become less important when we realize that the people society considers "least" are actually greatest in God's eyes.

In this story, Jan tells how her husband bucked social expectations in order to help her follow God's call:

> The power of professional status is not easily relinquished, but David Fairchild made that choice. He was a tenured university professor with a reputation for superior teaching and distinguished scholarship. He was the administrative leader of his department for seventeen years. Although he was still ten years from retirement age, he left that position of authority to follow me in ministry. I was called to a part-time pastorate in a small church 2,400 miles from where we had lived and worked for thirty years. After the move, David chose to continue teaching as a part-time university instructor. He has no rank, tenure, or authority. His income is about eleven percent of his former salary, and he receives no benefits. He chose to move down the social ladder.
>
> The role of a pastor's spouse is complex even when the spouse is female. When the traditional gender roles are reversed, the situation is even more complex. Although there is a growing acceptance of women as pastors, the acceptance of men as pastors' spouses has not kept pace.
>
> The change from university professor to pastor's spouse has not been easy for David. After a year of living in this different place, doing different work, and discerning his role in the church, there are still many unknowns and mixed blessings. His gifts for teaching and administration appear to be unappreciated. Although some people in the church still do not know how to respond to him, there have been positive changes. He has

become very active in the church, serving on committees and participating in worship. Some folks thank him enthusiastically for his contributions.

I, for one, cannot thank David enough for the changes he made so I could answer my call to ministry. I feel tremendous support from my spouse. For me, David's humility is an act of love that has enhanced our marriage.

This type of humility is costly, and it may seem foolish in a society where many people live for money, power, and prestige. The value of humility may not be evident to anyone except God. Even so, Matthew 18:1-4 assures us that God welcomes and honors people who accept the cost of humility.

We have seen that, for Matthew, humility means voluntarily going down the social ladder to the point that one accepts the low status of a child. Humility does not mean having a low opinion of oneself, although attitudes are certainly relevant. A key attitude is the desire to serve, but even service does not encompass all that Matthew's Jesus means when he says, "Whoever becomes humble like this child is the greatest in the kingdom of heaven" (18:4). If we have correctly interpreted the context of Matthew 18, childlike humility begins with the willingness to accept God's *grace*.

There is a subtle but real danger in the belief that service is the way to become great in God's eyes. As servants, we may imagine that we can earn God's favor by working harder, giving more, and requiring less for ourselves: "If God wants humility, then we will be humble until it hurts, until God finally notices just how humble we are!" But that sort of "humility" is really a form of pride in which the focus is on ourselves and our ability to please God.

When we find ourselves getting caught in that trap, we need to focus again on God's grace. We need to remember that God's love for us is already infinite and that nothing we can do will make God love us any more. We need to see the twinkle of humor in Jesus' eyes when he tells Peter how to find a coin for the temple tax. As we have seen, the message behind the humor is, "Lighten up! You cannot earn a place in God's family, but you are there already by grace." Jesus' example of a young child also suggests a connection between humility and grace. In our experience, children know how to accept good gifts, and we suspect the same was true in Matthew's time. Becoming humble like children means partly that we open our hands and hearts to receive gifts we have not earned. When adults strive for humility, we tend to miss the mark; but when we focus on God's grace, real humility can grow as the by-product of a deepening relationship with God. We can serve others more graciously because we are less distracted by the need to prove ourselves. We can risk moving down the social ladder because we know that God will continue to love and care for us, regardless of what happens.

Our final story about childlike humility does not come from friends in the Church of the Brethren, but from Michael Yaconelli, the pastor of a small church in the mountains of Northern California.

> A friend of mine spent the last year in and out of the hospital; the combination of a failing heart and cancer was almost too much to bear. His courage and determination caused him to bounce back from the edge of death, and he and his wife were able to celebrate Christmas together at home. I suggested that we celebrate Communion in their home on Christmas Day. Just before the appointed time, they called and asked if we could wait another hour because their grandson, his girlfriend, and her two boys from a previous marriage would like to take Communion as well. I walked into their small home to find everyone seated at the dining room table—Grandma and Grandpa filled with anticipation; grandson, girlfriend, and two boys noticeably nervous.
>
> After placing the bread and wine on the table, I asked if there were any questions before we started. The eleven-year-old boy, Joshua, asked if he could sit in on the Communion.
>
> "Of course," I said and checked to see if his mother agreed. She did. After the words of institution, I began to pass the bread and wine around the group.
>
> "May I take Communion?" Joshua asked.
>
> "Sure," I said, "Do you understand what all of this means?"
>
> The grandson interrupted, "Yes, he does. I explained it to him."
>
> Joshua took the body and blood of Christ, and as I was preparing to say the final prayer, he blurted out, "Sir, how can you hear God speak to you?"

Story Starter: Humility

Here are some suggestions for a church group that would like to practice humility more intentionally. The group could be a Sunday school class, a study group, a youth group, or a church committee. First, since we have seen that humility and voluntary service are closely related, invite one or two people with experience in a volunteer service program to speak with your group. Ask them to address their service in terms of humility. Did their experience change their concept of humility? What did they learn about the people and the culture with whom they lived and worked? What did they learn about themselves through the experience? Do they believe they have changed because of the experience?

For another angle on this topic, discuss ways in which your church has humbly served others in the past. When has the church reached out to individuals or groups considered unimportant by the world's standards but great in God's eyes? As you remember examples of service by the church, discuss them in terms of the questions you have asked of the volunteer service worker. What did members of the church learn about the people with whom they lived and worked through their outreach efforts? What did the church learn about itself through these experiences? Did the church change its understanding of humility because of this work?

Next, explore "new" ways in which your church can demonstrate humble service today. You may want to begin by identifying people in the community who are usually ignored or treated as unimportant. Then think of ways that you might recognize and serve them. Before deciding on a particular project, be sure to consult with some of the people you seek to serve. If possible, involve them in planning and carrying out the project. Try to think of a project that is new for your church, but not necessarily one that has "never been seen before." Does your Habitat for Humanity chapter need a sponsor for their next home? Has the economy created a local underclass of recently unemployed who need temporary shelter your church could provide? Is there a nonprofit agency seeking a partnership for urban redevelopment in the area around your church? How can you join with others in serving and honoring the most vulnerable people in your community?

As you identify, plan, and carry out a service project, be alert for examples of greatness as it is defined in Matthew 18:1-4. Were you able to honor some of the people in your community who are usually considered unimportant? Were there people among you who voluntarily accepted the role of a servant? Questions like these can help to renew the vision behind your project, and they can point toward new stories about humility.

Where this question came from I have no idea. I paused for a minute and said, "Well, Joshua, if you listen very carefully, you will know when God speaks to you. It may not be an audible voice, or it might not happen right away. But if you really listen, you will hear God speak." The trouble with children is they believe you. Immediately, Joshua squeezed his eyes, scrunched his body into listening mode, and started listening. I had given Joshua the adult answer to his question, never expecting him to put the answer to the test so soon.

"I heard Him!" Joshua yelled. "I heard God speak!"

I honestly don't think any of us in the room really believed Joshua heard God speak. We were trying to be nice, but we weren't expecting God to actually show up. "What did He say?" I asked. I was patronizing him, fully expecting some childish response.

Joshua looked straight into my eyes, his own eyes wide with wonder. "He said, *'Don't forget Me!'* "[18]

God chose to speak through Joshua with a message for the whole family and their pastor.

Like Joshua, the adults featured in this chapter show in various ways the kind of humility that grows from an awareness of God's grace. It is, we believe, the humility modeled by Jesus and by the child in Matthew 18:1-4. It is characterized by humble service and by a willingness to move down rather than up the social ladder. It is the primary mark of greatness in God's reign.

Questions for Discussion

1. Write a one-sentence definition of humility. After reading this chapter, has your understanding of humility changed? How?
2. What attitudes are necessary to be humble? What attitudes conflict with humility?
3. Why does Jesus use children as examples of humility? What does the example of the child in 18:1-4 contribute to your understanding of humility?
4. According to the authors' interpretation of Matthew 18:1-4, greatness in God's reign involves voluntarily moving down the social ladder. What might that mean to you personally? Have

you chosen to move down the social ladder? Could you do so in the future?

5. The authors state that there are subtle dangers in the belief that service is the way to greatness. Do you agree? Describe any dangers as you understand them.

6. The disciples in Matthew's story need to change their hearts and priorities. They need to concentrate on "getting into the reign of heaven" rather than "being the greatest in the reign of heaven." Do you consider this advice relevant for modern-day disciples? If so, how? How might following this advice affect your priorities?

NOTES

1. The themes of the five long teaching sections are: (a) the righteousness of people who will enter the reign of heaven (Matt. 5–7); (b) instructions for the disciples on how to proclaim the reign of heaven (Matt. 10); (c) parables of the reign of heaven (Matt. 13:1-53); (d) the greatness in the reign of heaven (Matt. 18); and (e) the final consummation of the reign of heaven (Matt. 24–25).

2. Terence J. Keegan, "Introductory Formulae for Matthean Discourses," *Catholic Biblical Quarterly* 44 (1982), 429.

3. For various perspectives on the theme and structure of Matthew 18, see William G. Thompson, *Matthew's Advice to a Divided Community, Mt. 17, 22–18, 35* (Rome: Biblical Institute Press, 1970), 242-44; W. D. Davies and Dale C. Allison, Jr., *A Critical and Exegetical Commentary on the Gospel According to Saint Matthew*, vol. 2 (Edinburgh: T & T Clark, 1991), 750; and other works reviewed in Daniel W. Ulrich, "True Greatness: Matthew 18 in Its Literary Context" (Ph.D. diss., Union Theological Seminary in Virginia, 1997), 16-31.

4. Matthew uses "the kingdom [reign] of God" in place of "the kingdom [reign] of heaven" in 6:33; 12:28; 19:24; and 21:31.

5. Richard B. Gardner, *Matthew*, Believers Church Bible Commentary (Scottdale, Pa.: Herald Press, 1991), 84.

6. Note that Matthew 16:18 can be translated, "I will continue to build my church."

7. Thompson, *Advice*, 98-99.

8. See Thomas Wiedemann, *Adults and Children in the Roman Empire* (New Haven: Yale University Press, 1989), 32, 39; Susan Dixon, *The Roman Family* (Baltimore: The Johns Hopkins University Press, 1992), 131; and Larry O. Yarbrough, "Parents and Family in the Jewish Family of Antiquity," *The Jewish Family in Antiquity*, ed. Shaye J. D. Cohen, Brown Judaic Studies 289 (Atlanta: Scholars Press, 1993), 48.

9. Robert H. Smith, *Matthew* (Minneapolis: Augsburg Press, 1989), 112.

10. Donald B. Kraybill, *The Upside-Down Kingdom* (Scottdale, Pa.: Herald Press, 1978), 258-290.

11. Dorothy Jean Weaver, "Rewriting the Messianic Script: Matthew's Account of the Birth of Jesus," unpublished paper presented at the Society of Biblical Literature Annual Meeting, Washington, D.C., 20-22 November 1993.

12. Alma Moyers Long, quoted in James H. Lehman, "The Spirit that Gave Birth to BVS," *Messenger* (July 1998), 15.

13. Ted Chambers quoted in Lehman, "BVS," 17.

14. Alma Moyers Long, quoted in Lehman, "BVS," 18.

15. Lehman, "BVS," 12-18; Donald F. Durnbaugh, *Fruit of the Vine: A History of the Brethren, 1708–1995* (Elgin, Ill.: Brethren Press, 1997), 492.

16. Tom Benevento, *Inwardly Rich, Outwardly Simple: Reflections of a Volunteer in Guatemala* (Elgin, Ill.: Brethren Volunteer Service, [1998]), n.p. Benevento's diary covers September 1991 through May 1998.

17. Norman L. Harsh, e-mail communication with Jan Fairchild on June 22, 2000.

18. Excerpted from *Dangerous Wonder: The Adventure of Childlike Faith* by Michael Yaconelli copyright 1999, 36-37. Used by permission of NavPress, www.navpress.com. All rights reserved. Emphasis original.

4

Welcome for Little Ones
Matthew 18:5-6

⁵ Whoever welcomes one such child in my name welcomes me. ⁶ If any of you put a stumbling block before one of these little ones who believe in me, it would be better for you if a great millstone were fastened around your neck and you were drowned in the depth of the sea.

The Biblical Story

In our study of Matthew 18:1-4, we saw that Jesus gives the disciples a challenging answer to their question about greatness in the reign of heaven. The greatest people in God's eyes are those who become lowly like children, following Jesus' example of humble service. This radical concept of greatness required further explanation. Like the disciples in the story, Matthew's readers needed to know in practical terms how they could live out the upside-down values of the reign of heaven.[1] Matthew begins this explanation in 18:5-6 with the message that disciples of Jesus are called to welcome children and other needy people in his name.

We have already noted that Matthew 18:5-35 presents a series of elaborations on the theme stated in 18:1-4. These elaborations are woven together so well it is sometimes hard to know where one ends and another begins; nevertheless, verses 5 and 6 belong together. In the original Greek they are joined by a conjunction meaning "but," which emphasizes the contrast between welcoming "one such child" and putting a stumbling block before "one of these little ones." The promise in verse 5 and the warning in verse 6 are two sides of the same coin.[2]

The shift from "one such child" to "one of these little ones" suggests that Matthew has more than literal children in mind, although they are also included.[3] In Matthew 10:42, Jesus describes the twelve disciples as "these little ones." The meaning of "little ones" is debated,[4] but an important clue is that Matthew associates "little ones" with "sheep," especially in the parable of the stray sheep (18:10-14; also see 26:31; Zech. 13:7). Jesus calls the disciples "little ones" just when he is sending them out "like sheep among wolves" (10:16). Meanwhile, Matthew uses "sheep" to describe people who are not yet disciples. For example, Jesus sees that the crowds are "harassed and helpless like sheep without a shepherd" (9:36), and he sends his disciples first "to the lost sheep of the house of Israel." It appears, then, that "sheep" and "little ones" are metaphors with similar meanings. Both describe people of any age who are vulnerable in the sense that they need protection, leadership, hospitality, or healing.

If this interpretation of "little ones" is correct, then people who are not yet disciples can also be "little." The phrase "little ones who believe in me" is usually understood as an exclusive reference to disciples, but even that is not certain.[5] The verb translated "believe" is closely related to a Greek noun meaning "faith" or "trust." In Matthew's story, the most shining examples of faith in Jesus are not the disciples, but other characters who come for healing. These characters include a centurion (8:10), people who carried a paralyzed man (9:2), a woman with a hemorrhage (9:22), and a Canaanite woman (15:28). The child in 18:1-4 also demonstrates trust in Jesus by coming when called; yet the text does not indicate that the child has become a disciple. The message of Matthew 18:5-6, then, is that vulnerable people should be welcomed in Jesus' name, whether they are already disciples or not.

This message is related to the overall theme of Matthew 18, because hospitality is one of the ways in which people show who is important to them. If the disciples in the story remain arrogant, they may snub people who appear to be beneath their status. If the disciples repent and become humble like children, they will be free to welcome and serve their lowly peers in keeping with God's priorities. Children and other "nobodies" will be their honored guests.

We have seen that hospitality played an important role in early Christian missions and in the circulation of Matthew's story, so it is not surprising that the story mentions rewards for people who welcome missionaries. For example, Matthew 10:13 implies that whole households will be judged "worthy" or not, based on whether they welcome the disciples whom Jesus sends. These missionaries will represent Jesus, who will be with them in spirit. Therefore, Jesus promises, "Whoever welcomes you welcomes me, and whoever welcomes me welcomes the one who sent me" (10:40).

The disciples are the ones who need hospitality in Matthew 10, but the situation is reversed in Matthew 18:5.[6] Now Jesus is challenging the disciples to welcome others as they would like to be welcomed. This challenge is relevant both for the disciples in the story and for Matthew's readers. The disciples in the story still have a child standing among them; only now it appears that Jesus is giving them a kind of test. How will these ambitious men respond? Will they reject the child, offer a warm welcome, or simply ignore the intrusion? Will they continue to dwarf the child, or will someone bend down for an eye-to-eye conversation? This test is crucial because it shows whether the disciples have adopted Jesus' scale of values. The disciples have confessed that Jesus is the Messiah, but they have not yet accepted Jesus' *way of being* the Messiah. Jesus has chosen to be humble and vulnerable like a child. In order to welcome Jesus fully *as he is*, the disciples must be willing to stoop and welcome a child. Otherwise, Jesus will remain something of a stranger in their midst.

Jesus' promise in Matthew 18:5 is relevant in yet another way for the disciples in the story. Jesus knows he will not be physically present with the disciples much longer, and he is counting on them to welcome and serve needy people in his absence. Only recently, some of the disciples had failed to heal a child while Jesus was elsewhere (17:14-20). The problem, according to 17:20, was the disciples' insufficient faith. Therefore, it is appropriate for Jesus to remind the disciples that he will be present whenever they welcome someone in his name.

The phrase "in my name" may carry several meanings at once. On one hand, it indicates the reason why the disciples would welcome someone. They are acting *because of* Jesus.[7] The same phrase could also indicate the source of the disciples' authority. They are *empowered by* Jesus to welcome and serve others. Matthew's Jesus often refers to his name in connection with a promise that he will be present with the disciples (18:5, 20; 28:19). If the disciples learn to trust that promise, they will be better prepared for Jesus' death and resurrection.

"Whoever" in Matthew 18:5 is a powerfully inclusive word, and Matthew uses it to include readers in Jesus' promise to be present in the act of hospitality. Many of Matthew's earliest readers heard the story because they had already welcomed a missionary. The story would have encouraged them to invite others who needed hospitality. Matthew assures these readers they can count on Jesus to be present with their guests.

Of course, hospitality might have been costly as well as rewarding for Matthew's readers. In the Jewish and Greek cultures of the first century, the expectations of hosts were rather demanding. At the very least, hosts normally offered their guests water for washing their feet, conversation, food, and a place to sleep. If guests were sick or injured, they could expect care until they got well. Hosts also had the duty to protect their guests from danger, even to the point of dying for them. Meanwhile, guests owed loyalty and respect to their hosts, along with a willingness to return the favor when needed.[8] If a host only welcomed folks who could reciprocate, then the demands of hospitality might be manageable; but the task of caring for the neediest people would have been as endless in Matthew's day as it is in ours.

Hospitality for children had its own costs and rewards. One of the sad realities of Matthew's time (and ours) was that many children needed homes. Orphans were common in an age when the average life expectancy for both men and women was around twenty years. In addition, it was not unusual for Gentile fathers to reject unwanted children (especially girls) and leave them to die. Several ancient authors found it remarkable that Jews did not share this practice. If an abandoned baby was found alive, she could be taken and raised as a slave. A few survivors were lucky enough to be legally adopted as children or given freedom as adults.[9] Matthew 18:5 implies that abandoned children should not be exploited as slaves, but welcomed as if they were Jesus.

In a world as dangerous as Matthew's (and ours), hospitality required trust on both sides. Guests trusted their hosts to provide a safe and nurturing space. Hosts meanwhile trusted that their guests would not violate that space, but would show gratitude for the gifts they had received. Matthew encourages both hosts and guests with the promise that Jesus will be present among them. There are risks in hospitality, because either the guest or the host can violate the other's trust, but the risks of failing to practice hospitality are even greater. If people keep only to themselves, they lose the chance to care for one another. Friendship and love become difficult, if not impossible. It is no coincidence that Matthew views faith or trust as a requirement for healing. Without some degree of trust, people who are ill cannot accept the care they need. Furthermore, when disciples fail to practice hospitality, they miss opportunities to share the gospel with others and to experience Christ's presence in that encounter.

According to Matthew 18:6, the worst alternative to practicing hospitality is putting "a stumbling block before one of these little ones who believe in me." These words echo Leviticus 19:14: "You shall not revile the deaf, or put a stumbling block before the blind." In Matthew, however, the offense is far more serious than the prank prohibited in a literal reading of Leviticus. A "stumbling block" in Matthew's story can be anything that tempts people to reject God's will or God's Son. For example, Peter becomes a "stumbling block" for Jesus when he stands in the way of Jesus' journey to Jerusalem (16:23). The disciples also try to keep children from reaching Jesus by speaking sternly to parents (19:13). Clearly, the disciples in the story need to be warned about putting stumbling blocks in the way of others.

The conclusion of verse 6 warns of a horrible punishment for anyone who places a stumbling block in the way of a little one who trusts in Jesus. Without specifically naming this punishment, Jesus implies that it will be worse than drowning in the deepest part of the sea with a huge millstone (literally "a donkey's millstone") hung around one's neck. In Matthew's story, the sea symbolizes chaos and death, and the disciples are terrified of drowning there (8:23-27, 32; 14:22-33).

Even though the sea inspires terror, it is also a place where Jesus reveals his power and grace. When Peter begins to sink in the sea, he cries out "Lord, save me!" and Jesus reaches out to catch him (14:30-31). That rescue foreshadows Peter's whole experience with Jesus. Peter starts well but falters because of his inadequate faith. He becomes a stumbling block for Jesus and eventually denies knowing him. By the end of the story, Peter probably deserves to drown with a millstone hung around his neck, but what he receives instead is forgiveness and restoration. In the context of Matthew's story, the reference to drowning in 18:6 carries a double meaning. On one hand, it shows that Jesus takes very seriously the need to protect little ones who have faith in him. At all costs, his disciples should avoid doing anything that would cause them to lose that faith. On the other hand, the sea is a reminder that Jesus has the power to save even the worst offender. Lapses in hospitality are within the scope of his grace.

Meanwhile, people who practice hospitality in Jesus' name are also recipients of grace. The point of Jesus' promise in 18:5 is *not* that the disciples will *deserve* to have Jesus as their guest if they simply welcome one needy person. The presence of Jesus is a gift, just like his forgiveness.

Our Stories

Judging from the stories that have been shared with us, many people experience Christ's presence and blessing during simple acts of hospitality. We have heard from hosts who suddenly recognized Jesus in their guests. We have also heard from guests who deeply appreciated a welcome they received, sometimes many years earlier. In some cases, the host never knew how much their loving care meant to those who received it.

Duane Grady remembers the welcome he and other children received from Wilbur J. Miller, a member of the church where Duane grew up:

> The most powerful person at the South Waterloo Church of the Brethren was an aged gentleman who hung up children's coats. Mr. Miller was not much taller than many of us, and he was frail and stooped over. He always stood by the coatrack which was in the Sunday school wing of the church. As children came to Sunday school, he would take their coats and hang them up. He was by the coatrack again as children left for home, giving them their coats and helping to put them on.
>
> What made this action powerful for us kids was that it was not an official role. Mr. Miller volunteered to do it, and when he died it was not continued by anyone else. I don't remember any words that he used, but he obviously expressed warmth and caring. He taught us through actions that kindness matters and that we mattered. His actions were lived-out theology. When we heard the story of Jesus welcoming the children we thought of him.
>
> At that time, children were not deemed very significant in the operation of the institution. There was no children's time during worship, and most of what happened there went right over the heads of kids. I can't recall any message from a sermon or wor-

ship service, but I have vivid and clear images of Mr. Miller
taking my coat Sunday after Sunday.[10]

Duane gives a mixed review of the welcome that he experienced as a
child in church. He felt welcome in Sunday school but not in worship.
Unfortunately, Mr. Miller's wonderful hospitality ended with his death.

Like Jesus' teaching in Matthew 18:5-6, Duane's story can challenge congregations to welcome children and others more warmly. Many
of us believe that our congregations are warm and friendly, but the
more important question is, How are we perceived by the people God
calls us to welcome? If long-time members could experience our congregations from the perspective of children and newcomers, we might
see a need for significant changes, both to widen the church's welcome
and to remove potential stumbling blocks. Memories of our first experiences with the congregation might be helpful, but an even better approach may be to listen carefully to the experiences of children and
others who have come to the congregation more recently.

A helpful resource for congregations that want to practice biblical
hospitality is *Widening the Welcome of Your Church: Biblical Hospitality and the Vital Congregation*, by Fred Bernhard and Steve Clapp.[11]
Fred is pastor of the Oakland Church of the Brethren, which has practiced a vision of biblical hospitality for many years. Members at the
Oakland congregation had great reservations about evangelism if it
meant abruptly asking others whether they were saved, but those same
members felt comfortable with a call to practice hospitality. As Fred
and other leaders began to emphasize biblical teaching about hospitality, the congregation responded. Training workshops encouraged members to view strangers as potential friends. Members were given specific assignments, such as greeting people in the church parking lot
and at the door. Each Sunday, designated members came prepared
to invite visitors to their homes for lunch. Deacons encouraged listening both to visitors and to inactive members. Sunday school classes
and other groups within the church developed plans for reaching
out to inactive members and potential members. During the initial
three months of the hospitality emphasis, Sunday school attendance
increased by thirty-six percent and worship attendance by nineteen
percent compared with the same period during the previous year. Increases have continued year by year.[12]

Although numerical growth can be a byproduct of hospitality, Fred and Steve emphasize that biblical hospitality is not a strategy for church growth but simply a way of loving and accepting others. The acceptance is unconditional:

> Hospitality offers space for the stranger where change can take place. Hospitality does not require change before extending acceptance. Thus, hospitality stretches us and pushes us to see others more as Christ would—to recognize the presence of Christ even in those who are very different from ourselves.

If the church's hospitality becomes artificial, manipulative, or self-serving, then guests will tend to withdraw as soon as they perceive that the welcome is not real. On the other hand, the church's hospitality is not a substitute for calling people into discipleship.

> Accepting the stranger or any other participant in the Christian community is not synonymous with condoning or accepting every aspect of his or her lifestyle or behavior. Ultimately, we welcome the outsider to become our friend and walk with us on the road to Christian obedience and maturity.[13]

In other words, biblical hospitality involves both the acceptance of others as they are *and* the hope for mutual friendship and shared discipleship. That friendship has the potential to change everyone involved.

Fred celebrates the potential relationship between hospitality and discipleship by telling this story that he calls "unusual":

> There is a couple who are now deacons. He's a professional person, and two of his employees, who are members at Oakland, were talking one day about the love feast that was going to take place that night, on Maundy Thursday. And he said to these two employees, "Pray tell, what in the world is love feast?" And they proceeded to explain love feast to him. [Love feast is the traditional way to celebrate communion in the Church of the Brethren. It includes worship, feetwashing, and a meal along with the bread and the cup.] Then the employees said, "Better yet, why don't you come and see for yourself?" And just out of plain curiosity he came and was so impressed by the service and by what he experienced that he went home and told his wife,

"We're going to church there next Sunday." And he brought his wife and two children and they've been here ever since.

Later on, they gave their own testimony, which we have on video. She said, "When we came to Oakland the first Sunday, it's such a large church that people literally had to go out of their way to say hello to us, and they did, and made us feel welcome." He said this was the first place he had ever been where he saw what he perceives as the New Testament being lived out.[14]

The story is unusual not because hospitality led to discipleship, but because that process happened so quickly and easily.

It is not surprising that a congregation would welcome a professional couple, especially when they come so eagerly and even record their compliments on videotape; but not every guest is so easy to welcome. When Fred was asked about the limits of hospitality at Oakland, he said that the greatest barriers are wealth and poverty. As for the wealthy:

A guy sold his business for seventeen million. All of a sudden he's a rich man and everybody knows it. He goes and buys a three million dollar house. Everybody says, "Let's all stare." When he shows up in church everybody wants his money, but they don't want him because they don't how to treat him. They don't know how to act toward a person they think has more than they have. Now if that person had grown up Brethren he would have done something else. He would have hidden his wealth. And we wouldn't have known that he was that rich, and we would have said, "Come on. We'll be glad to have you around."

In speaking about the poor, Fred referred to Head Start, a federally funded preschool program that uses the church's educational wing:

We have tried over and over to try to find a way to welcome and put out the welcome mat for Head Start families, who tend to be impoverished, and that's been a difficult step. And what we're discovering is it's not only difficult for us, but it's difficult for them. Those of us who are putting out the mat think, "We can accept whoever you'll send us." They think, "We can't perform according to your standards." It has to do with hygiene, with the kind of cars people drive, with education. Some can't read or write, but we assume when we print worship folders that people here are literate. We assume a lot.

A couple of years ago in an inquirers' class. I casually mentioned Noah as one of the biblical models of faith. And one of the class members stopped me. "Fred, Noah who?" And all of a sudden it clicked with me, this person has no concept at all of any biblical character, including Noah. And I said, "You never heard the story of Noah, did you?" And this person said, "I don't know what you're talking about." Most of us in the Christian church assume that the people God is sending to us will have some understanding of biblical faith. And when we get an illiterate, it takes time and patience to disciple that kind of person not only in biblical knowledge, but in what loyalty means, in what accountability means, in what integrity means, the whole bit. If we're really serious about welcoming all kinds of people, we've got to change.[15]

Fred raises important questions about the changes that congregations may need to make in order to welcome all kinds of people: Whom are we excluding from worship or other church activities when we assume that everyone who comes will know how to read? How can we plan so that children and adults who are not comfortable reading will feel at home and able to participate?

Through most of its history, the church has used art, drama, and a wide variety of symbols to communicate the gospel with nonreaders. In some traditions, including the Church of the Brethren, hymns were "lined" for the benefit of those who could not read a hymnal. (The leader sang a line and then everyone repeated it.) Today many North American congregations are experimenting with simpler, more repetitive music with rhythms that appeal to the young. Some of us still prefer the rich poetry of longer hymns; others like a mixture of styles. If we seek to practice biblical hospitality, however, the key question is not "What style do I like?" but "How can I welcome and nurture others?" Change and renewal are likely to result whenever biblical hospitality is a top priority for the church.

Biblical hospitality includes welcoming people in worship and nurturing them spiritually; but, for many people physical needs take priority. Therefore, it is important to note that hospitality includes caring for guests in whatever ways are most needed. It is hard to argue with James 2:15-16, which reminds us, "If a brother or sister is naked and lacks daily food, and one of you says to them, 'Go in peace; keep warm and eat your fill,' and yet you do not supply their bodily needs, what is the good of that?" Likewise, Matthew 18:5-6 does not limit the range of needs that the disciples may be called upon to meet as they welcome children and other little ones in Christ's name.

For an example of hospitality that meets physical as well as spiritual needs, we can turn to Christ House, a thirty-two-bed medical facility serving homeless people in Washington, D.C., since 1985. Although hospitals give emergency care to homeless people, a lack of continuous care means there is no place to recuperate and no treatment for chronic illnesses such as AIDS, cancer, or heart disease. Christ House provides ongoing medical care along with referrals for other services. Out of 231 people treated in 2001, 80 percent went on to suitable, long-term housing.[16] Christ House also provides free showers and changes of clothes to the people who line up daily. A clear witness to everyone who comes by Christ House is a bronze statue of Jesus sculpted by Jimilu Mason. Jesus kneels before a basin dressed in modern clothes that look tattered, as though he might be homeless. His hands are outstretched to wash a foot, but the space between them is empty. He looks up, inviting anyone and everyone to have their feet washed.

The statue offers hospitality in the name of Jesus, but the staff and residents of Christ House are the ones who make that offer real through daily hard work. Joy Horner Kauffman, who served as food service coordinator at Christ House in 1994–95, shares this story of mutual hospitality:

> I met Christ in a Safeway store today. He offered to bear my cross. It really caught me off guard; you see, it's not so easy to recognize Him. But today He made Himself so . . . I don't know, so real. It was as if He picked me out of a crowd and decided I was worthy of His compassion.
>
> I was working when it happened—ironically enough, for a place called "Christ House," a medical recovery facility for homeless ill men in Washington, D.C. Even at that, I almost missed Him. I needed food for the evening meal, and was standing at the deli counter to ask about a donation of meat, when He

walked up behind me and spoke to my turned back. Many a drunken mumble have fallen on these ears, was my thought upon hearing his slurred speech.

I turned to look for the source of the sound. He was a small man with humble shoulders, Latino, with a soiled shirt and tattered trousers. The rims around his eyes were red. I've come to think of this as a symptom of alcoholism, or maybe it's from life on the streets in this nation's capital. I looked away and in that glance noticed a few other customers looking at me. You see, He was a Latino and had crossed into that huge sphere of space we of European descent consider personal. Unconsciously, yet nervously, I considered shopping in another part of the store. I turned and walked, keenly aware He was following me.

I stood staring at packaged meat, knowing He is still behind me. My mind flashed back to a difficult conversation I had the weekend before. I had been with a friend from college with whom I used to go to church. Her life and mine are currently on different tracks, and bridging our differences has been challenging. We are just three years out of school and already she owns a house in the suburbs and is planning with her husband for their children's college education (even though because of careers they plan not to have children for at least seven years). Meanwhile I run the kitchen at a hospital for homeless men, live in the District of Columbia and thrive on discussions of ways to "live simply."

But the line from the conversation that haunted me now was one I had not even spoken for fear of creating more tension. The thought was, "How will we respond to Jesus when He asks us, 'What have you done for the least of these?' "

God, I thought, here I am ignoring the very one. How will I respond? So I turned and looked Him in the eye. "Sir, were you speaking to me?"

"Lady, I don't wanna bother you. I saw you talking to that man and he didn't wanna help and I knew you was askin' and I wanna help you, Lady."

His words revealed that this man had in fact followed me from my work and He knew I needed help. When I left the building, I had walked past the homeless men lined up for free showers and changes of clothes. I hadn't noticed Him in the crowd but he must have been listening when I asked Alfredo for help.

Alfredo is a person with whom communication is always a challenge, due to both my rudimentary Spanish and his failing brain cells from years of alcoholism. I had asked Alfredo for help carrying bags from the store. He either hadn't understood or didn't feel like helping because he wasn't budging. So I gave up, assuring him it was no problem, that I would go alone.

So here I was—standing next to the meat counter in Safeway speaking with a man whose appearance has already caused one of those coded intercom announcements in stores that tell employees "Dirty drunk harassing customer in aisle 13." There were already two Safeway aprons on the scene. They stood back, respecting the sphere, thinking we were together.

"Lady," he continued, "I don't mean to scare you, but I didn't like how that man was treating you, asking for help and him not helping you."

He wiped his irritated eye with the back of his leathery hand, and I glimpsed the results of years of hard labor in the sun.

"Thank you," I muttered, still a little taken aback. "You were in front of Christ House? I didn't see you."

His head dropped a bit. "I was waiting for a shower. I don't wanna lose my place, but you was needin' help. I can carry your bags."[17]

Joy's story is a powerful reminder that Jesus is present in the "least of these." When our eyes and hearts are open, we can see him almost anywhere.

The joyful surprise of meeting Jesus in a stranger helps to explain why hospitality can be habit-forming. Many habitual hosts tell about lifelong friendships or treasured memories that began with the simple act of welcoming a stranger. These rewards are so rich that they outweigh the costs and risks of hospitality.[18]

To call Naomi West a "habitual host" would be an understatement. For decades, Naomi and her late husband Guy West have welcomed a stream of refugees and other guests from around the world. They began resettling refugees in the 1950s during Guy's pastorate at the York Church of the Brethren in Pennsylvania. When they retired to Bridgewater, Virginia, Naomi volunteered to coordinate refugee resettlement for Shenandoah District of the Church of the Brethren. While

Naomi preached hospitality in churches around the district, she continued to practice hospitality at home. In addition to resettling refugees, she has participated in Servas International, Habitat Your Way, Mennonite Your Way, and other hospitality networks. Her guest books contain hundreds of names from thirty-nine different countries, but they are not just names to Naomi. They are people she loves and who love her in return. Many call her "Mother West," and her refrigerator is literally covered with photographs of a huge adopted family.

In a three-hour conversation about her experiences in practicing hospitality, we questioned Naomi about her experience as a host, but her answers always focused on her guests. Showing one photo after another, she told about the persecution and violence that many of them had escaped, their difficulties in adjusting to a new land and culture, their interesting quirks, their successes and failures, their jobs, and their families. We wondered how a new generation of Christians would develop the habit of hospitality. How does one become a "Mother West"? Naomi did not answer that question directly, except to say that she learned hospitality from her parents. The real answer became clear, however, with every story she told. The way to become a "Mother West" is to focus attention on others instead of on oneself. Naomi is genuinely interested in every person she encounters, and her attentiveness opens the door for deep and enduring relationships. Her hospitality is rooted in humility, the value that is most central to Matthew 18.

Matthew 18:5 claims that we welcome Jesus whenever we welcome a needy guest in his name. That claim has not gone out of date. People like Wilbur Miller, the Oakland Church of the Brethren, Joy Horner Kauffman, and Naomi West have tested it and found it true. May it prove true in all of our lives as we seek to practice discipleship according to Matthew 18.

Questions for Discussion

1. What is your understanding of the word *hospitality*? How does it compare with the ideas put forth in this chapter?
2. In Matthew's story, Jesus challenges the disciples to welcome others as they would like to be welcomed. How do you like to be welcomed?

Story Starter: Hospitality at Church

Consider carrying out this project with a group from your church. Preferably the group will include people with diverse ages and life experiences. The group will need to meet at least three times for a project that will last ten to twelve weeks.

At the first meeting, take stock of the ways your church practices hospitality. How are strangers welcomed? Do specific greeters or ushers provide the primary or first welcome to strangers? Do others welcome people? Does the church's hospitality to strangers include any of the following: an invitation to a member's home for a meal or a meal at a restaurant after church; a follow-up welcoming letter or phone call; a small gift of fresh baked goods? What other types of hospitality have you practiced? On a typical Sunday, how many people would greet a stranger at your church? Compare the estimates and identify a list of people who are natural greeters in your church. Discuss why some people greet strangers at church while others do not.

Also at its first meeting, your group will need to plan tasks to be completed during the next three to four weeks. If possible, identify several people who started attending the church recently, and plan for group members to interview them. Ask what it is about your church that made them feel welcome or less than welcome. Also, each member of the group should plan to visit one or two other churches. The visitors should take notice of ways other churches practice hospitality. How were they welcomed? What practices might be good for your church to try?

After all the visits are completed, the group should meet again to discuss their findings. As part of this discussion, prayerfully identify one or more hospitality practices that the group feels called to adopt in your congregation. When the group agrees on some good possibilities, they should share their ideas with others in the church, including people whom you would like to be involved.

If others in the church agree, work to implement the group's ideas for several weeks at least. If possible, check with visitors who experienced the church's new hospitality practices. How welcome did they feel at your church? Did they decide to return? The third meeting is for reflection and evaluation of what has happened. During that meeting, the group can develop a recommendation about whether to continue its ideas or try some other form of hospitality.

3. How do you extend hospitality to others? Describe your personal style of hospitality. Do you extend hospitality to strangers? Are you hospitable in one way at church and in another way at home? What are the differences?

4. Do you have a memorable experience of receiving or giving hospitality, a time perhaps when the presence of Jesus was especially apparent in your encounter with a stranger? Please share your experience with others.

5. How do your perceptions of the "other person" affect your hospitality? Do your perceptions of others limit the range of people to whom you give hospitality, or do they limit the kinds of hospitality you extend?

6. Are there people who would feel unwelcome in your church? What perceptions of the place and the people might make them feel unwelcome?

NOTES

1. Donald B. Kraybill, *The Upside-Down Kingdom* (Scottdale, Pa.: Herald Press, 1978), 275-76.

2. William G. Thompson, *Matthew's Advice to a Divided Community, Mt. 17, 22–18, 35* (Rome: Biblical Institute Press, 1970), 103-7.

3. W. D. Davies and Dale C. Allison, Jr., *A Critical and Exegetical Commentary on the Gospel According to Saint Matthew*, vol. 2 (Edinburgh: T & T Clark, 1991), 761. On the inclusion of literal children, see Frederick Dale Bruner, *Matthew: A Commentary* (Dallas: Word Publishing, 1990), vol. 2, 642.

4. See Dorothy Jean Weaver, *Matthew's Missionary Discourse: A Literary-Critical Analysis* (Sheffield: Sheffield Academic Press, 1990), 119.

5. Eduard Schweizer, *The Good News According to Matthew*, trans. David E. Green (Atlanta: John Knox Press, 1975), 365.

6. Thompson, *Advice*, 103-4, 107-8.

7. Weaver, *Missionary Discourse*, 119-20.

8. J. T. Fitzgerald, "Hospitality," *Dictionary of New Testament Background*, eds. Craig A. Evans and Stanley E. Porter (Downers Grove, Ill.: InterVarsity Press, 2000), 522-25.

9. Thomas Wiedemann, *Adults and Children in the Roman Empire* (New Haven: Yale University Press, 1989), 17, 36-37, and *Greek and Roman Slavery* (Baltimore: The Johns Hopkins University Press, 1981), 118-19; Ross S. Kraemer, "Jewish Mothers and Daughters in the Graeco-Roman World," *The Jewish Family in Antiquity*, ed. Shaye J. D. Cohen (Atlanta: Scholars Press, 1993), 108.

10. Duane Grady, e-mail message to Dan Ulrich, 10 October 2000, and in an unpublished manuscript, "Disciplines for Church Life: Good News for Committed Christians," 35.

11. Fred Bernhard and Steve Clapp, *Widening the Welcome of Your Church: Biblical Hospitality and the Vital Congregation*, 3rd ed. (Fort Wayne, Ind.: Christian Community; Elgin, Ill.: Brethren Press, 1999). A study guide is included.

12. Bernhard and Clapp, *Widening the Welcome*, 28-31.

13. Bernhard and Clapp, *Widening the Welcome*, 33.

14. Personal interview with Fred Bernhard at the Oakland Church of the Brethren in Darke County, Ohio, September 4, 2001.

15. Personal interview with Fred Bernhard on September 4, 2001.

16. Introduction to Christ House, a ministry of the Church of the Savior, published on the Internet by Christ House at http://www.christhouse.org. Accessed on October 5, 2001.

17. Joy Horner Kauffman, "I Met Christ at Safeway," published on the Internet by Christ House at http://www.christhouse.org/Stories/safeway.html. Accessed on October 5, 2001. This story first appeared in *a Common Place* 2 (June 1996), 21.

18. Although there are real risks in extending hospitality to strangers, Bernhard and Clapp point out that the news media's focus on violent crime has led many people to be more fearful than necessary. See Fred Bernhard and Steve Clapp, *Hospitality: Life Without Fear. Finding Meaning and Purpose in a Fearful World* (Fort Wayne, Ind.: LifeQuest, 2000), 7-15.

5

Radical Self-Discipline
Matthew 18:7-9

⁷ Woe to the world because of stumbling blocks! Occasions for stumbling are bound to come, but woe to the one by whom the stumbling block comes! ⁸ If your hand or your foot causes you to stumble, cut it off and throw it away; it is better for you to enter life maimed or lame than to have two hands or two feet and to be thrown into the eternal fire. ⁹ And if your eye causes you to stumble, tear it out and throw it away; it is better for you to enter life with one eye than to have two eyes and to be thrown into the hell of fire.

The Biblical Story

We have seen that Matthew 18:5-6 presents a sharp contrast between two ways of treating children and other needy people. Welcoming them is a way to welcome Jesus, but putting a stumbling block before a needy person who trusts Jesus is an offense worthy of a terrible punishment. The seriousness of the offense is apparent when we remember that in Matthew's story a stumbling block can be anything that tempts someone to reject God's will or God's Son.

Matthew 18:7-9 expands on the warning about stumbling blocks in 18:6. The tone remains stern as Jesus rapidly "zeroes in" on the causes of stumbling, moving from a broad view of the world (18:7a), to the individual (18:7b), to parts of the individual (18:8-9). The message for Jesus' disciples is clear: They must practice radical self-discipline in order to eliminate all causes of stumbling. Otherwise, they may fail to enter life in God's reign and become obstacles to others as well (18:8-9; 23:13).

In Matthew 18:7, Jesus uses emotionally charged language to warn about God's judgment against people who cause the spiritual downfall of others. "Woe" translates a word that was used by mourners at the death of a loved one. When prophets in the Old Testament pronounced "woes" over Israel and other nations, they were imitating the cries of a mourner. They lamented God's coming judgment as though it had already occurred. Jesus utters two such cries in Matthew 18:7, first over the world and then over the individual who causes others to stumble.

The context for these laments will become clearer as we study some other references to "the world" and "stumbling" in Matthew's story. In Matthew 13, Jesus tells two parables about fields and then interprets them privately for the disciples. In the parable of the sower, seeds fall on different types of ground (13:1-9, 18-23). The rocky ground represents persecution, which causes new believers to "fall away," or literally "to stumble" (13:21).[1] Meanwhile, in the parable of the weeds (13:24-30, 36-43), the field represents the world, where the Son of Man sows good seed but the devil sows weeds. The weeds represent stumbling blocks and evildoers, which God's angels will gather and burn as part of the final judgment (13:41). Taken together, the interpretations of both parables suggest that stumbling blocks will remain in the world as a threat to the disciples' mission until the final judgment. The world will continue to produce stumbling blocks much as a field produces rocks and weeds. Persecution, in particular, will test the disciples' long-term commitment to Jesus and his mission.

According to Matthew 13:39, the ultimate cause of stumbling blocks in the world is Satan. In Matthew's story, the world belongs to God, but Satan claims control over it (4:8-9), wielding enormous, though temporary, power. Satan's power explains why "occasions for stumbling are bound to come" (18:7),[2] but it does not excuse the world for giving Satan room to operate. Jesus knows how devastating the world's stumbling blocks can be for disciples and other vulnerable people. He also knows that God will judge the world for producing stumbling blocks on Satan's behalf. No wonder Jesus is weeping like a prophet!

The second woe in Matthew 18:7 is for any human being whom Satan uses to produce a stumbling block in God's world. The word "but" here does not cancel the woe for the world, but it shows that the next woe is the real point of the saying. Even though the world as a whole deserves judgment because of stumbling blocks, an individual

who causes the downfall of others is particularly worthy of Jesus' prophetic lament. In other words, human beings are still responsible for
their choices that allow stumbling blocks to arise. If the disciples had
no power to resist Satan, then there would be no point in exhorting
them to do so.

In Matthew's story, Peter is the human character who most fits the
description, "the one by whom the stumbling block comes" (18:7). When
Peter attempts to block the journey to Jerusalem, Jesus recognizes the
work of Satan and declares, "Get behind me, Satan! You are a stumbling block to me" (16:23). Jesus' words echo his rebuke of Satan in
the wilderness (4:10) and remind readers that Jesus was tempted to be
the Messiah in ways that did not involve a cross. In 16:23, Satan uses
Peter to continue tempting Jesus. Peter, however, is speaking as a representative of all the disciples, any of whom might be used by Satan.
Therefore, Jesus' rebuke in 18:7b challenges all the disciples in the
story (and all readers) to consider whether they could be a stumbling
block for others.

If the answer is yes, Matthew 18:8-9 urges further self-examination
and correction. An unstated assumption linking 18:8-9 with the preceding verses is that someone who stumbles may cause others to trip as
well. Therefore, the disciples must avoid stumbling at all costs, both
for their own sakes and for the sake of others. Anything that repeatedly
causes them to stumble—even a foot, hand, or eye—must be cut off
and thrown away.[3]

Taken literally, these instructions would be gruesome enough for a
horror movie, but they are not intended literally. They mean that the
disciples must eliminate any attitude or habit that keeps them from
following God's will. Ambition, arrogance, and inadequate faith are
some of the attitudes the disciples in the story need to "cut out" and
discard. In 18:3, Jesus tells the disciples they must change and become
like children in order to enter life in the reign of heaven. The surgery
prescribed in Matthew 18:8-9 is another way to speak about repentance and radical change.

People who undergo radical surgery are usually trying to avoid worse
health problems or even death. Likewise in Matthew 18:8-9, the horrible alternative to self-discipline is to be thrown into "fiery Gehenna."
"Gehenna" is derived from the Hebrew name for a valley near

Jerusalem. It was the city's main garbage pit and a place where infants once burned as sacrifices to foreign gods.[4] According to Matthew, God will use Gehenna as a place of punishment for evil people after the final judgment (5:22, 29-30; 10:28; 23:15, 33). Although this view of God may be troubling, it shows that God takes sin very seriously. Matthew emphasizes the grace of God also, but it is not cheap grace. God's grace is especially precious to people who believe in God's judgment.

Matthew 18:8-9 is sometimes interpreted as a call to excommunicate sinful members from the body of Christ, but there are good reasons to doubt that interpretation.[5] First, there is no other passage in Matthew that refers to the church as the body of Christ. That idea comes from Paul rather than from any of the Gospels. In addition, the pronouns and verbs in Matthew 18:8-9 are all singular in the original Greek. Plural forms would be more appropriate if the call was for collective action by the church. Furthermore, if Matthew 18:8-9 were about church discipline, it would be harsher than 18:15-17, where the goal is not to cut off church members but to win them back. Instead of contradicting the teaching about church discipline in 18:15-17, Matthew 18:8-9 adds something else, namely, a strong emphasis on self-discipline. The same emphasis appears in Matthew 7:5: "First take the log out of your own eye, and then you will see clearly to take the speck out of your neighbor's eye." We should not be surprised, then, that Matthew 18 includes a saying about self-discipline (18:8-9) before sayings about correcting others (18:10-17). Finally, Matthew 18:8-9 repeats a saying found in 5:29-30, where the context clearly requires an individual interpretation.

Since Matthew intended for his story to be read aloud, repetition was a way to make sure that listeners did not miss essential points. Judging from the repetitiveness of 5:29-30 and 18:8-9, Matthew must have thought his readers needed to hear about self-discipline. There are also good reasons for Jesus to repeat this saying to the disciples in the story. The warning about stumbling takes on new meaning after Peter's mistake in 16:22-23, and the disciples are also coming closer to the time when they will stumble because of Jesus' arrest (26:31). The Greek grammar suggests that stumbling is a real problem for them.

There is a close relationship between the repeated warnings about stumbling and the overall theme of Matthew 18, which is that humble people are the greatest in the reign of heaven. If arrogance is a primary cause of stumbling, removing that attitude will lead to growth in humility. Meanwhile, humble people are the ones most likely to engage in honest self-examination, to admit their weaknesses, and to seek God's help in making the changes that will allow them to avoid stumbling. Becoming humble is therefore the crucial change that makes healthy self-discipline possible. Finally, self-discipline helps create an environment where children and other "little ones" can be safe. Since the "little ones" are great in God's eyes, their protection is a top priority.

Our Stories

Stories about self-discipline can be difficult to share and even more so to publish; nevertheless, when we share our struggles honestly, we usually find that we are not alone. Temptation is a universal experience, and everyone but Jesus has sinned, so we have no reason to condemn one another. Instead, we can listen and share with compassion.

Both authors of this book have had experiences where we felt called by God to change. In Dan's case, one of those experiences was life-threatening:

> On October 12-13, 1993, I had two kinds of surgery, and only one of them was physical. I was in a Ph.D. program and felt enormous pressure because of the candidacy exams that lurked on my calendar only a few weeks away. During a five-month marathon of preparing for those exams, I had neglected many other things, including relationships with my wife, Paula, our children (ages one and four at the time), and God. By early October I was also ignoring my body, and I dismissed a dull pain in my stomach as a symptom of the stress I was under. A flu-like fever came next, but it, too, was ignored for as long as possible. I simply had no time to be sick. By the time I saw a doctor, my appendix had ruptured, resealed, and refilled. Fortunately, a surgeon removed it before it could rupture again. He told me later, "You really dodged a bullet."
>
> On the day after surgery, my pastor anointed me for healing. Antibiotics and pain medication were both pumping through my body, but I was alert enough to realize that I needed more help

than surgery or medicines could provide. I needed to be cleansed of the sewage that was threatening my physical life, *and* of the sin that was fouling up my most important relationships. The anointing was like a second surgery, but the result was a deeper healing than I had thought possible. I confessed my sins of pride, perfectionism, and bottled anger. I experienced God's forgiveness and felt God's presence again. God gave me a deep sense of protection and peace. Even though I was still very sick, I knew nothing could ever separate me from God's love.

It was weeks before I regained my physical strength and months before I took the exams, but none of that mattered because my priorities were different. The surgeon was wrong when he said that I had dodged a bullet. What really happened was that I stopped dodging God. I continue to struggle with the sins that I confessed at that anointing, but at least I know where to find help.

Jan has struggled recently with her role in the call and discernment process at the congregation she pastors:

When I began as pastor of the Springfield Church of the Brethren in August 2000, the church had been without a pastor for nearly six years. During this time, the membership of about forty people had ministered to one another, and they had completed a long process of self-examination and discernment to determine the church's mission. When I accepted the call to be their pastor, I knew I was entering an unusual situation. I was excited about the challenges and opportunities of ministering with people who had a strong commitment to deepen their relationships with God and one another. I was also anxious about ministering with a congregation that had been without a pastor for so long.

In October, the church embraced my suggestion that we begin a process to discern members' spiritual gifts and call them to serve. For a month the worship services and sermons focused on call and discernment, and everyone was encouraged to complete a survey of the congregation's spiritual gifts. At the end of that month, the congregation called two people and the pastor to form a discernment committee. This committee in turn called people to serve on the various church committees, using information gleaned from the survey of spiritual gifts. This approach to "doing church" was very new for many people, but they accepted it with a great deal of trust and enthusiasm.

A year passed. It was time to call a new person to the discernment committee and to continue the process of calling people to positions in the church. The preparation was similar to the first year, and the results looked similar initially; but as the discernment committee started to contact people, some friction began to surface. Some people expressed their primary concern as, "Who will be on the committee with me?" Or, "I can't be on the committee if so-and-so is on the committee." One person demanded to be placed on a committee which the discernment committee had *not* recommended. The people who expressed these concerns did not appear to be focusing on their gifts. The discernment committee was becoming frustrated, and I was questioning the entire process. I began to take the negative feedback too personally.

As I considered the situation, I realized that there were some things I could have done differently. I had put most of my energy into the outward results of the discernment process, namely, getting people into place in the church structure. I had not given enough attention to the inner work of prayer and discernment that was essential as we sought to match people with opportunities in which they could express their spiritual gifts.

My self-examination raised some difficult questions: Was I trying to control this process? *Yes!* Was I encouraging people to find the God-given freedom to express their unique spiritual gifts? *Not really*, even though that was my intention.

In retrospect, I realize that I could have led the discernment committee differently. We could have prayed more together and talked more deliberately about the way the Spirit was leading us to make our decisions. When problems surfaced, we could have spent more time discerning how we should react to people's concerns.

My struggles with these issues have led me to the conclusion that I must pay consistent attention to my own inner work. I continue to explore through prayer and meditation what it means to discern. In part it means releasing my desire to control the outcome and trusting that God creates order out of chaos. If I do not live my gifts from the inside out, can I hope to minister to others on a similar journey?

This story is incomplete. The congregation will have more opportunities to explore what it means to be a spiritual, gift-guided body; I will have more opportunities to practice prayerful self-discipline and trust in God. We plan to officially evaluate the discernment process next year.

As Jan's story illustrates, one of the key ingredients in faithful ministry is self-discipline. Self-discipline is essential not just for pastors, but also for any Christian who attempts to serve others in some way. It means, in part, that we are able to learn from mistakes and make changes where needed. Since we do not automatically recognize when our actions have fallen short of God's will, we need to set aside time for prayer, Bible study, and reflection. Those quiet times give us a better chance to hear God, and they renew our energy to obey.

To state this idea in another way, self-discipline at its best involves a continuous cycle of action and reflection. Even though our ability to know and obey God's will is imperfect, we often need to act based on our limited understanding. Those experiences provide material for reflection, which is a chance to discern more fully what God is doing and how we are called to participate. We can then apply what we have learned in our next attempt at action.

For another example of action followed by reflection, we turn now to a story from Bethany Williams, who was in Brethren Volunteer Service at the time:

A man brought his pregnant girlfriend and her son from a previous marriage to the homeless shelter where I was working. As I completed their intake information, it became apparent that they needed to go to the medical clinic. It was my responsibility to drive them. Although I was unaware initially that the man had been drinking, I learned later that he was intoxicated. As we approached the van, the man's body language seemed threatening. He loudly swore a response to another resident's simple question, and he forcefully threw a cigarette on the ground before entering the van and slamming the door.

At the clinic I sat in the waiting room observing the couple's actions and expression. Both were silent and tense. The face of the twenty-one-year-old woman looked aged and withdrawn—

similar to a movie I had seen where one of the female characters was a victim of domestic violence. The man tried to grab a piece of paper from his girlfriend. She resisted and he grabbed her. She turned away, pulling her arms to her chest and crossing her legs to protect herself. She stood up to switch chairs, and he grabbed her wrist and twisted her body around as she struggled to get free. She broke loose as another resident screamed, "Don't you dare touch her!" The man raced out of the room, slamming the door; and as the door closed, the woman burst into tears crying, "Why does he always have to do this to me?"

At that moment I was sure that the man was capable of violence, capable of returning and harming his girlfriend or anyone else in the room. I had to do something. I became a child with frozen eyes. A million thoughts raced through my mind, the only part of me not paralyzed by what I had seen. I could not imagine what he must do to her outside the public setting of a hospital clinic. My previous notions of being a calm, articulate person who could handle any crisis unscathed disappeared. My idealistic thoughts about having the power to save the world from suffering all by myself were forgotten. I had thought of myself as a person who in this situation would have called 911 immediately with a detailed description of the situation and would have had the registration clerk call security to see that the man did not escape the building. All I could do was dial the number of the shelter where I worked, and even when I spoke to the familiar voice of a co-worker, I could barely articulate who I was, let alone explain what I needed.

After several broken sentences that could barely pass for English, my co-worker dialed 911 for me. Five minutes later, the police entered the waiting room and interrogated me. I could only answer a few of the questions confidently. The woman denied having been abused in any way, and she was upset that her boyfriend had to leave the shelter because she was afraid no one would take care of him. For days later, whenever I remembered that night, all I could think about was how weakly I responded and how paralyzed I felt. I was not the strong hero I thought I was. But maybe God had a different lesson for me to learn that night. As I reflected on my previous attitudes about myself, I saw much arrogance and selfishness. I was quite naive to think that I alone could put an end to a domestic violence situation that had probably been part of a much larger cycle. To put myself above the victim by thinking that I could "save her" was quite condescending. In a way, it was claiming to be a godlike figure in my mere human body. God probably saw that my genuine concern for humanity was clouded over with self-righteousness.

Perhaps if I were able to remain present and in the moment, without drowning in the surrounding emotions, I could have responded earlier and quicker, maybe even preventing the man from grabbing his pregnant girlfriend. But God showed me that night that caregiving does not consist of picking up people and carrying them on my shoulders to a place where I think they should be physically and emotionally. Rather, I must stand with people on their level, admitting that I still have a long way to go in my spiritual journey. I need to learn to be silent and genuinely listen to the needs of the individuals and learn from them in the process as fellow human beings. It is only then that caregiving is possible.[6]

Bethany may be too hard on herself in this story. Few would interpret her motive as "selfishness," for many capable people have felt "paralyzed" while watching a violent incident. Nevertheless, Bethany has named some important changes that she would like to work toward. She wants to be less naive and more aware of her limits. She wants to serve others without imagining that she can be savior of the world. She wants to "be silent and genuinely listen" to the needs of others with sincere caring but without condescension or self-righteousness. Bethany appears to be moving toward these worthy goals through a process of self-discipline.

Self-discipline can be especially difficult when we need to change ingrained habits or addictions. In that case, even to recognize our need for change is a major accomplishment, and long-term recovery can be a daily struggle. Addictions such as alcoholism and codependency often contribute to the kind of situation that Bethany describes. Alcohol reduces people's inhibitions, making them more likely to express anger violently. Codependency leaves people feeling unworthy or unable to leave an abusive relationship.[7] Alcoholics and codependents usually need outside help in order to move toward recovery, and the same is true of many other addictions.

Unfortunately, getting help is almost impossible until one recognizes the need for it, and the addictions of others are much easier to diagnose than our own. We are often blind to the stumbling blocks that Satan is using against us; otherwise they would not be as effective in alienating us from God. One question to ask as we try to diagnose ourselves is, What habits would we be unwilling or unable to give up even if we knew that God required us to do so? Those habits may well be addictions, especially if we use them to cover the pain of broken relationships, including a broken relationship with God. Overeating, overwork, human approval-seeking, sexual infidelity, gambling, and unnecessary consumer spending are only a few of the addictive behaviors that abound in North America. If you suspect that you may have one of these addictions (or a different one), then it is time to seek help, both from God and from knowledgeable people.

Fortunately, help is available for those who want to change. Certainly God is ready to help. God also may work through medical professionals or peer support groups. Alcoholics Anonymous has helped many alcoholics control their addiction through a combination of intensive peer support and a well-known twelve-step process. There are similar twelve-step programs for people recovering from a wide variety of addictions.

The Twelve Steps of Alcoholics Anonymous closely mirror biblical teachings about repentance, reconciliation, and grace. Taken together, they are a story written by the earliest participants in A.A. about their experience of self-discipline empowered by God:

1. We admitted we were powerless over alcohol—that our lives had become unmanageable.

2. Came to believe that a Power greater than ourselves could restore us to sanity.

3. Made a decision to turn our will and our lives over to the care of God as we understood Him.

4. Made a searching and fearless moral inventory of ourselves.

5. Admitted to God, to ourselves and to another human being the exact nature of our wrongs.

6. Were entirely ready to have God remove all these defects of character.

7. Humbly asked Him to remove our shortcomings.

8. Made a list of all persons we had harmed, and became willing to make amends to them all.

9. Made direct amends to such people wherever possible, except when to do so would injure them or others.

10. Continued to take personal inventory and when we were wrong promptly admitted it.

11. Sought through prayer and meditation to improve our conscious contact with God as we understood Him, praying only for knowledge of His will for us and the power to carry that out.

12. *Having had a spiritual awakening as the result of these steps, we tried to carry this message to alcoholics and to practice these principles in all our affairs.*[8]

We believe that these twelve steps are consistent with the gospel. Indeed, they seem essential for any Christian who seeks to recover from an addiction or to prevent one.

Self-discipline may seem like a dreary subject consisting of a series of internalized rules and demands; nevertheless, the purpose of self-discipline is not to take away our joy in living. Most of the negative rules in scripture are like fences designed to keep us from falling into a pit. The pit is what would take away our freedom. The purpose of the fence is to help us stay free so that we can enjoy life as God intended from the beginning. The positive demands in scripture are especially challenging because we can never claim to have fulfilled them completely; there is joy, however, in knowing that God can use our small efforts for a purpose that is larger than ourselves. A deepening

Story Starter: Twelve-Step Support Group

This project is recommended for a group of five to seven people with the goal of exploring self-discipline together, using a method based on the Twelve Steps of Alcoholics Anonymous. Members of the group should covenant to meet together at least weekly for three months and to keep what is said at their meetings confidential. Everyone should be encouraged to share freely and listen compassionately. The group may be able to invite an experienced facilitator to lead the whole series of meetings or simply to introduce the twelve-step process at the first meeting.

Vernon J. Bittner's *You Can Help with Your Healing: A Guide for Recovering Wholeness in Body, Mind, and Spirit* (Minneapolis: Augsburg-Fortress, 1994) is an excellent source book for this project. Bittner devotes a chapter to each of the twelve steps, and each chapter includes scriptural references, personal examples, and stories. The study guide is sufficiently detailed that even someone with no experience with twelve-step programs can successfully facilitate a group project. Other resources your group may find helpful include: J. Keith Miller, *A Hunger for Healing* (HarperSanFrancisco, 1992) and *A Hunger for Healing Workbook* (HarperCollins, 1992); and Tim Timmons, *Anyone Anonymous* (Fleming H. Revell, 1990).

Once the group completes the twelve-step program, take time to reflect together on this way of practicing self-discipline. Were members able to complete the twelve steps with help from one another? How, specifically, did members demonstrate radical self-discipline as taught in Matthew 18:7-9? In what ways did your understanding of twelve-step programs change through this experience? Did the group's experience enhance your appreciation of twelve-step programs generally, or diminish it? Would you recommend a twelve-step program as a model for others who seek to explore radical self-discipline?

awareness of God's grace will greatly increase our joy. One of the most frequent commands in the Bible is "Rejoice!" God does not want us to postpone joy, but to experience it now, even in the midst of our current struggles.

Taken in context, Matthew 18:7-9 does not call for dreary self-discipline. Indeed, dreariness may itself become a cause of stumbling, an attitude we need to discard, just like its cousin, arrogance. Both involve taking ourselves too seriously. The Pharisees in Matthew's story are an example of dreary discipline. They focus on legal details to the extent they forget to practice and celebrate God's mercy (23:23-24). Likewise, dreary Christians today may quietly convince their neighbors and even their loved ones that Christianity is not for them. Richard Foster emphasizes this point in the final chapter of his classic book on spiritual disciplines: "Celebration is central to all the Spiritual Disciplines. Without a joyful spirit of festivity, the Disciplines become dull, death-breathing tools in the hands of modern Pharisees. Every Discipline should be characterized by carefree gaiety and a sense of thanksgiving."[9]

Our most basic complaint about dreary self-discipline is that it is not radical enough. The word *radical* comes from the Latin word for "root." It literally means "getting to the root of the matter." The root of positive Christian discipline is a loving, nourishing relationship with God. We need that relationship in order to fill the void that many try to fill through addictions, material wealth, or power. When our relationship with God is growing, God's immense love for the world will crescendo inside us and echo outward. We will have every reason to rejoice.

Questions for Discussion

1. Have you ever stumbled in your faith? Were you aware of stumbling at the time? Describe the circumstances. Could your stumbling have caused others to stumble? Can you describe how that might have happened?

2. Describe the meaning of a "stumbling block" as you understand it, and give some examples you have observed in the world where you live. In what ways do these "stumbling blocks" cause people to become alienated from God?

3. What does self-discipline mean for you? Name and describe someone who exemplifies good self-discipline. What personal characteristics are most important for self-discipline?

4. List some benefits of self-discipline. What is the relationship between self-discipline and health? How might self-discipline help prevent or overcome stumbling in Matthew's sense of that word?

5. Do you agree with the authors that humble people are most likely to practice self-discipline? Why or why not?

6. What do you think of the twelve steps that are the basis for Alcoholics Anonymous and related programs? If you have attempted to follow them, did you find the experience helpful? How are the steps similar to, or different from, your understanding of Christian repentance and reconciliation?

7. The authors draw a contrast between dreary self-discipline and self-discipline that is joyful because it is rooted in a growing relationship with God. Have you experienced this difference personally? How do you combine self-discipline with joy?

NOTES

1. The same Greek verb (*skandaliz,* cause to stumble) is used in Matthew 13:21 as in Matthew 18:6-9.

2. W. D. Davies and Dale C. Allison, Jr., *A Critical and Exegetical Commentary on the Gospel According to Saint Matthew,* vol. 2 (Edinburgh: T & T Clark, 1991), 764.

3. The verb for "cause to stumble" (*skandaliz*) is in the present tense, which in Greek usually indicates that the action is continuous or repeated.

4. Jeremiah 7:30-34; 19:6-9. Also, Blaine Charette, *The Theme of Recompense in Matthew's Gospel,* Journal for the Study of the New Testament Supplement Series 79 (Sheffield: Sheffield Academic Press, 1992), 141.

5. Scholars who interpret Matthew 18:8-9 as a call for church discipline include: Alan Hugh McNeile, *The Gospel According to St. Matthew* (London: Macmillan, 1938), 262; Dan O. Via, "The Church as the Body of Christ in the Gospel of Matthew," *Scottish Journal of Theology* 11 (1958), 271-86; and J. C. Fenton, *The Gospel of St. Matthew* (Baltimore: Penguin Books, 1963), 294. For individual interpretations, see Eduard Schweizer, *The Good News According to Matthew,* trans. David E. Green (Atlanta: John Knox Press, 1975), 365; Davies and Allison, *Matthew,* vol. 2, 765; and Richard B. Gardner, *Matthew,* Believers Church Bible Commentary (Scottdale, Pa.: Herald Press, 1991), 276.

6. Bethany Williams, e-mail communication with Janice Fairchild, November 3, 2000.

7. For more information on co-dependency, see Melody Beattie, *Codependent No More: How to Stop Controlling Others and Start Caring for Yourself* (San Francisco: Harper & Row, 1987).

8. Alcoholics Anonymous, accessed on the Internet at http://www.alcoholics-anonymous.org, November 20, 2001. The italics are original.

The Twelve Steps are reprinted with permission of Alcoholics Anonymous World Services, Inc., (A.A.W.S.). Permission to reprint the Twelve Steps does not mean that A.A.W.S. has reviewed or approved the contents of this publication, or that A.A.W.S. necessarily agrees with the views expressed herein. A.A. is a program of recovery from alcoholism only. Use of the Twelve Steps in connection with programs and activities that are patterned after A.A., but address other problems, or in any other non-A.A. context, does not imply otherwise. Although Alcoholics Anonymous is a spiritual program, A.A. is not a religious program, and use of A.A. material in the present connection does not imply A.A.'s affiliation with or endorsement of any sect, denomination, or specific religious belief.

9. Richard J. Foster, *Celebration of Discipline: The Path to Spiritual Growth*, 20th anniv. ed. (San Francisco: HarperCollins, 1998), 191. The chapter is titled "The Discipline of Celebration."

6

Compassionate Searching
Matthew 18:10-14

¹⁰ Take care that you do not despise one of these little ones; for I tell you, in heaven their angels continually see the face of my Father in heaven. ¹² What do you think? If a shepherd has a hundred sheep, and one of them has gone astray, does he not leave the ninety-nine on the mountains and go in search of the one that went astray? ¹³ And if he finds it, truly I tell you, he rejoices over it more than over the ninety-nine that never went astray. ¹⁴ So it is not the will of your Father in heaven that one of these little ones should be lost.

The Biblical Story

In Matthew 18:10-14, Jesus continues to elaborate on the theme announced in 18:1-4, which is that humble people are great in God's reign. We have already seen some implications of that theme in our study of 18:5-9. The disciples are to mirror God's view of greatness in the welcome they extend to "little ones," meaning vulnerable adults or children. But biblical hospitality involves more than welcoming people; it means welcoming people *into a safe space*. Therefore, Jesus goes on to warn against putting a stumbling block before "one of these little ones who believe in me." The disciples are in danger of stumbling and of becoming stumbling blocks for others, so Jesus urges them again to repent and discipline themselves. They must "cut out" dangerous attitudes like arrogance, overconfidence, and lack of trust. Disciples who practice that sort of discipline will be prepared to welcome and serve "little ones" as the greatest in God's reign.

In Matthew 18:10-14, Jesus teaches the disciples to do more than wait for "little ones" to arrive. The disciples have been called to share in Jesus' mission and to follow his example, which means they must search urgently and compassionately for people who might otherwise be lost. The parable of the stray sheep in verses 12-13 is the heart of this section, since verses 10 and 14 frame and interpret the parable. (We will not consider verse 11 here, since it is missing from the earliest manuscripts and from most modern versions. It was probably a copyist's addition to the text, based on Luke 19:10.)

The warning against despising "one of these little ones" (18:10) helps link verses 10-14 with the preceding call for self-discipline and with the overall theme that humble people are great in the reign of heaven. The word translated "despise" means to look down arrogantly on someone. If the disciples hold a superior attitude toward "little ones," they show a complete misunderstanding of Jesus and an urgent need for repentance. "Little ones" may seem insignificant, but they are of utmost importance to God.

As further evidence of God's priorities, Jesus first gives the disciples a glimpse of the heavenly throne room, where angels wait to do God's bidding. The angels assigned to protect "little ones" are especially powerful because they have constant access to God's face.[1] Other Jewish writers went so far as to name the archangels who continually intercede for God's suffering people and who will eventually carry out the final judgment by throwing the wicked into Gehenna (the burning garbage pit outside Jerusalem).[2] Matthew evidently assumes this background without giving names. The disciples should think twice before they antagonize such powerful angels.

In verses 12-13, the scene shifts abruptly from heaven to earth, where a shepherd has come up short in his nightly counting of the flock. The grammar of Jesus' question assumes that the obvious answer is yes, of course a shepherd would leave ninety-nine sheep on the hills in order to scour the countryside for one stray.[3] Since a real shepherd probably would not leave the rest of the flock unattended, some scholars have concluded that the parable is about the "foolish grace of God," who acts in surprising ways to rescue those who have strayed.[4] God's grace certainly *is* amazing; nevertheless, the parable does not state that the ninety-nine are left unattended. A real shepherd would normally leave his flock in the care of someone else, and Matthew's readers would probably have assumed some such arrangement. The point of the parable is not that the shepherd takes unusual risks with the ninety-nine, but that the shepherd gives priority to searching for one stray.[5]

Of course, there is a crucial difference between a stray sheep and a lost one. A stray is not finally lost until it dies or until the shepherd gives up the search. There is no guarantee that the search will succeed, but the shepherd goes on anyway, taking enormous pains in the hope of finding the stray before it dies. If the search does succeed, there is no thought of punishing the sheep, only joy at finding it safe and sound.

Matthew 18:14 interprets the parable by suggesting that the shepherd's search mirrors God's concern for people who have strayed from the reign of heaven. After the abrupt transition from heaven to earth in 18:12, readers are led just as abruptly back to God's heavenly court, the same scene described in 18:10. Literally, verse 14 could be translated, "There is no desire before your Father in heaven that one of these little ones should be lost." In other words, the decision in God's heavenly court is unanimous. Everyone there agrees that even one stray human is precious.

Although verses 10 and 14 connect the shepherd with God, other parts of Matthew's story show that the shepherd can also represent Jesus and his disciples. Matthew 2:6 announces that Jesus will "shepherd my people Israel," and Jesus fulfills that prophecy through his ministry of teaching, preaching, and healing. Jesus is a compassionate shepherd. He sees that the people of Israel are "harassed and helpless like sheep without a shepherd" (9:36), and he sends out the disciples as an extension of his ministry "to the lost sheep of the house of Israel" (10:6). Later he compares healing a crippled man to rescuing a sheep that has fallen into a pit (12:11). His question on that occasion is similar to the parable of the stray sheep: "Suppose one of you has only one sheep and it falls into a pit on the sabbath; will you not lay hold of it and lift it out?"[6] Although Jesus objects at one point that he was "sent only to the lost sheep of the house of Israel," he also has compassion on needy Gentiles (15:21-28). By the end of the story, he no longer tells the disciples to restrict their mission to Israel. They are to make disciples of all nations (28:19). The end of the story also shows Jesus acting as a shepherd for his followers. The men especially are scattered after Jesus' arrest, but he gathers them again on a mountain in Galilee (26:31-32; 28:10, 16-20).

These examples suggest that Matthew 18:10-14 should be interpreted in light of the shepherding theme that runs throughout the story. As we do this, three points deserve special emphasis. First, Jesus is the primary model for a disciple's work as a shepherd. During the same speech in which Jesus sends the disciples to search for "the lost sheep of the house of Israel," he declares, "It is enough for the disciple to be like the teacher" (10:25). The clear implication is that all disciples are called to share Jesus' concern for lost "little ones." In light of the example set by Jesus and the shepherd in the parable, the warning not to "despise one of these little ones" in Matthew 18:10 turns out to be a vast understatement. It means that the disciples must actively seek and love people who could otherwise be lost to God.

A second key point is that Matthew portrays the disciples as both shepherds (10:6) and sheep (10:16; 26:31). This double portrayal is realistic because the disciples are fallible human beings who will need to be rescued before they can rescue others. Even after the resurrection, when Jesus has regathered the eleven disciples and they are worshiping him, there is a striking note of realism. In the NRSV, Matthew 28:17 reads "some doubted," but the Greek could be translated simply "they doubted." Matthew is hinting that the disciples may fail again because of insufficient faith. The eleven are being commissioned to disciple all the nations, but they will also need to be discipled. The shepherds are also sheep.

Finally, Jesus is concerned about anyone who strays from the reign of heaven, not just about disciples who stray from the church. Earlier in Matthew's story, the phrases "Father in heaven" (18:10) and "the will of your Father" (18:14) are both associated with the reign of heaven (6:9-10). We have also seen that Matthew does not equate the reign of heaven with the church. Therefore, an interpretation of Matthew 18:10-14 that focuses only on stray church members is too limiting. In Matthew's story, all children of Israel are "heirs of the kingdom" (8:12), and those who have strayed from God's reign need to be brought back to their inheritance (10:6; 15:24). In addition, Jesus is concerned about people from other nations, including people who will be led astray from God's reign in the future (24:9-14, 24). The disciple's mission is to search compassionately for people who are already disciples of Jesus *and* for people who are not yet disciples. People in both groups need compassionate listeners, just as they need to hear the good news of God's grace. Pastoral care and evangelism go hand in hand.

Our Stories

In many congregations pastoral care focuses almost entirely on people who are active in the church. Sharing the gospel with people who have strayed from God's reign is usually more difficult, whether they are inactive members or people who have never joined a church. Some congregations accept the challenge of evangelism, and many of them are growing. Others have neglected this basic task; and, not surprisingly, their numbers have tended to decrease. In the Church of the Brethren, total membership has declined steadily since the early 1960s from a high near 200,000 to fewer than 140,000 in the year 2000. This trend has led to urgent calls for renewal through evangelism and church planting. Unfortunately, it is easier to talk about evangelism than to do it.

In an Evangelism Leaders Academy, Herb Miller quipped that too many congregations follow the Little Bo Peep approach to shepherding:

> Little Bo Peep has lost her sheep and can't tell where to find them.
> Leave them alone and they'll come home, wagging their tails behind them.

There are two main problems with this approach: It doesn't work, and it isn't what Jesus wants. Matthew tells us to imitate the Good Shepherd instead of Little Bo Peep.[7] The church must not be content with passive hospitality, imagining that people who need God will show up at church if we only wait long enough. A few may indeed show up, and we need to welcome them; but active, compassionate searching is essential if we are to fulfill the mission that Jesus has given us.

Studying Matthew 18:10-14 in context can help us to meet this challenge faithfully. One reason for discomfort with evangelism is that sometimes it is attempted without the humility taught in Matthew 18. The solution is not to neglect evangelism, but to do it in a way that is more consistent with Jesus' teaching and example. According to Matthew, Jesus' mission involves concern for whole people: their physical well-being and their relationships with God and other people. Jesus does not seek to dominate others but to serve them. If we also approach others humbly, we will be prepared to listen at least as much as we talk. Instead of presuming that we have a superior understanding of God, we will seek to build relationships in which we can share our faith and learn from the faith of others. Humble witnesses do not need to know the answer to every question that someone might ask. It is enough to admit that we do not have all the answers, but that we have found life in Jesus. Even the most saintly Christian is dependent on God's grace, and God can work through any sinner; therefore, we usually have no reason to decide in advance who is the stray sheep and who is the shepherd. The important thing is that we find the way home together.

Another cause of discomfort with evangelism may be a reluctance to visit door to door. For busy North American families, the visits conducted by Mormons, Jehovah's Witnesses, and other groups may feel like a rude imposition. Doors in North America tend to be locked, and the people inside are reluctant to open them for strangers. Again, the solution is not to reject (or neglect) evangelism, but to do it differently. In some settings, door-to-door evangelism may still be appropriate, but a better approach in North America may be to develop friendships intentionally with the unchurched people we already know. They may be neighbors, co-workers, classmates, or even relatives. We can begin by asking God to show us people who need to hear the gospel. We can then pray for those people daily and ask God for opportunities to share our faith with them. It is surprising how often such prayers are answered, perhaps because the act of praying makes us aware of the opportunities God was providing all along.

In Matthew 10:9-11, Jesus instructs the disciples to travel lightly from village to village and to accept the hospitality of a "worthy" household for as long as they remain in a village. As we have seen, that approach to evangelism was well suited to the Mediterranean culture of the first century A.D., where hospitality toward strangers was a central value and where whole households could be converted at once. The message of that passage today is not that we must all wander barefoot from city to city, but that we must all work urgently to share the good news of God's saving reign. Our methods need to be consistent with the gospel *and* with the culture of the people we are called to reach.

In January 2001, a group of students from Bethany Theological Seminary traveled to the Dominican Republic for a course in evangelism. The group received a warm welcome from Dominican sisters and brothers who were eager to show how they witness for Jesus Christ in their communities. One of the host congregations was the *Fuente de Vida* (Fountain of Life) Church of the Brethren in Los Guaricanos, an impoverished neighborhood near Santo Domingo. Pastor Diamira Berigüete began the congregation by preaching in the streets, visiting in homes, and welcoming people for worship in her own small home. The congregation now meets in a beautiful building but continues its tradition of street-preaching. On one Thursday afternoon, the North American visitors joined about twenty members of the congregation as they divided into groups and walked through the neighborhood. There were no closed doors; most people were sitting outside their small homes; and everyone who would listen received a short sermon about salvation, a spoken prayer, and an invitation to worship. The North American guests were amazed at the warm reception that almost everyone gave to this ministry. Students imagined doors slamming in their faces, but in the Los Guaricanos neighborhood people listened respectfully, even eagerly, to the gospel.

There are also many people in North America who would love to have a Christian visitor. To give just one example, Sarah's health no longer permitted her to run the small business that had been her life for forty years, so she sold it and moved across the state where she could be near her daughter. Except for her daughter's busy family, however, she knew no one. Intense pain kept her at home most of the time, and loneliness made the pain worse. Fortunately, Mary, a deacon from a nearby church, noticed that someone new had moved to the neighborhood. When Mary stopped by with a small housewarming gift, Sarah was obviously delighted. Mary kept coming; her visits were bathed in prayer; and the two women developed a strong, nurturing friendship. Sarah renewed her relationship with God, and whenever she was able, she accepted Mary's invitation to church. Eventually Sarah joined the church, and at the pastor's suggestion she got involved in a telephone ministry, calling others in the congregation who also struggled with loneliness.[8]

Both of the previous examples show that compassionate searching is a task for all Christians, not just pastors. The word *pastor* is Latin for "shepherd," and churches need ordained pastors who will act like the shepherd in Matthew 18:10-14. Matthew, however, makes no distinction between different categories of disciples. Every disciple is called to follow Jesus' example and share in his mission. New believers are often very effective in sharing their faith with others, both because of their enthusiasm and because they have relationships with people who are still outside the church.

The Easton Church of the Brethren has involved many members in sharing the gospel through drama and clowning. In the fall of 1990, for example, over forty members and friends of the congregation helped to produce a play by Paul McCuster titled *Snapshots and Portraits.*[9] Act One of this play presents the joys and frustrations of people living in various kinds of families. Sharon is a young, single woman sharing an apartment with a friend. Gloria is divorced and working hard to raise her son without the help of a father. Jim is a middle-aged man, recently widowed, who angrily bails out his son from another incident of drinking and driving. Joshua is a paralyzed stroke victim who lives in a nursing home and longs for a visit from his estranged son.

In Act Two, which is set in Jim's living room on Thanksgiving Day, the audience learns that all of these characters are related: Sharon and Gloria are Jim's daughters, and Jim is the son Joshua longs to see. Sharon and Gloria visit Jim for Thanksgiving, but the visit ends too soon. Jim feels terribly alone and powerless to deal with the struggles in his extended family. He receives a wonderful gift, however, as he daydreams a conversation with his late wife, Barbara. After listening to Jim's troubles, Barbara gently reminds him that he has never really been alone. God's love has always been the foundation of their family, and God is powerful enough to heal the hurts and bridge the chasms they are experiencing now. As Thanksgiving unfolds, Jim finds the strength to forgive both his father and his son. The love that binds his family together is visible again.

There were no dry eyes in the Easton congregation's packed sanctuary at the end of this powerful play. It was easy for the audience and the cast to identify with the characters, partly because some of the families connected with the church were facing similar situations. Although the congregation as a whole is loving and supportive, some members had stopped attending because of family conflicts or because they didn't feel comfortable in their parents' church. In that situation, *Snapshots and Portraits* was a wonderful way to share the gospel without preaching. God used that experience to heal relationships and bring some people back to the church.

We have said that the method of evangelism should be consistent both with the gospel and with the culture of those we are called to reach. This statement leads to a crucial question: *Whom* are we called to reach? Church growth experts have observed that it is easiest for the church to include new members who are culturally similar to the people already there.[10] If the goal of evangelism is to fill pews, then the logical conclusion would be for each church to focus its outreach on "people like us." Matthew, however, points to a different goal based on a different concept of greatness. According to Matthew 18:13, there is a huge party in heaven whenever anyone is found for God. The goal of evangelism is not to fill pews; it is to reach someone who could otherwise be lost. The greatness of a church is measured by its compassion, not its membership list.

Blaine Minor speaks passionately about the need for that kind of evangelism among the children he serves. Blaine is a chaplain and counselor in a state-run prison for youth ages thirteen to twenty-one in northern Illinois. In response to our call for stories about discipleship according to Matthew 18, he told about a teenager who had landed back in detention for the third time. When Blaine asked what had happened, the boy explained that both his grandparents were in the hospital, and he had to be there with them, so he skipped school. The boy's heart was in the right place, but he failed to check in with his parole officer, and the result was a warrant for his arrest. The whole situation could have been avoided with a phone call, but that kind of accountability is often difficult for teenagers who have essentially raised themselves. According to Blaine, "Latching on to Christianity is literally a matter of life and death for these kids."

In Blaine's experience it is not unusual for troubled children to accept Jesus as Savior and Lord; but, when they do, the crucial question is, What now? Children who accept Jesus need to be nurtured in a Christian community where members are at least as committed as the "brothers" and "sisters" in a street gang. Otherwise, the gang may be too tempting. Part of the solution, Blaine says, is for Christians to build relationships with troubled children and their families. For example, the church can reach out by providing quality childcare, or by making sure that people have transportation to visit loved ones who are in prison. As we build loving relationships and ask God for guidance, there will be opportunities to share the gospel in words as well as actions. Blaine knows from experience that reaching out to at-risk children and their families can be tough, thankless work, but he sees it as an essential aspect of discipleship according to Matthew 18. He would like more help from the church.[11]

If Christians hesitate to share the gospel with people who might otherwise be lost to God, one reason may be that we are afraid of failure. Earle Fike Jr., touched on that fear when he asked, "What if the lost sheep doesn't *want* to be found?"[12] A real shepherd might pick up the stray sheep and forcefully return it to the fold; but we are dealing with people not sheep, and people cannot be forced into a loving relationship with God. When people decide to reject the gospel, we can respectfully accept their choices without feeling we have failed. God works patiently in all kinds of circumstances, and God can use our apparent failures in ways we do not anticipate.

Mark Craddock, pastor of the Maple Grove Church of the Brethren, has shared this story about an apparent failure in evangelism:

> I am a volunteer at Prodigal's Community, a drug and alcohol rehabilitation center for hard-core offenders. Prodigal's Community treatment program requires a fifteen-month minimum stay. Most of the people in the program have been in other treatment facilities before they arrive at Prodigal's Community. Some of them have been in as many as thirty other facilities.
>
> Shortly after I began volunteering some eight years ago, the director, a Mennonite minister, asked if our church would consider doing a feetwashing service and allowing the residents to participate. We jumped on the chance to share this experience with them. I was asked to read the scripture. Before I started reading, the director invited anyone who was uncomfortable with this ceremony to just slide his or her chair back and not participate. As our pastor explained the feetwashing, one resident after another slid back. I thought surely they were just moving back to have more room to take off their shoes, but no, they wanted no part of the ceremony.
>
> I was at the table with one of our dearest deacons. We looked at each other, unsure what to do. I stood up, put on the apron, and went to his end of the table and washed his feet. Then we exchanged places and he came to my end of the table and washed my feet. We hugged, and he went to each of these men who had no understanding of this type of humility, pleading with tears in

his eyes to wash their feet. But they would have none of it. I was absolutely thrown for a loop! I looked around the room. Our congregants and the director had been the only participants. None of the men in the program had participated. I was sorely disappointed. I felt the whole thing had been a waste of time.

On the way home that night, my wife, Elaine, told me that a couple of the women had participated, but not all of them. I expressed my frustrations with what had happened. Elaine, the eternal optimist, said simply, "You never know what seeds were planted."

A couple of years later we attended Prodigal's Community's fifth anniversary party. Some of their graduates had been invited to share their testimonies at the celebration. One young woman recounted her experience in the program, recalling how she had been beaten down and felt she had no reason to live. She told us she had been ready to quit, to leave the program and return to the streets. But one night a group of Brethren came over and shared a feetwashing ceremony. She told how strange it felt to sit next to "church people" who loved her unconditionally for who she was, and to have her feet washed by them. She said that was the most meaningful thing that had ever happened to her. She said she knew then that God loved her and would help her get through the program. She stayed in the program, and became the first woman to graduate from Prodigal's Community!

I sat there with tears streaming down my face. I had thought our feetwashing experience had been a failure. God used it to turn someone's life around.[13]

Matthew 18:10-14 calls the church to search compassionately and humbly for even one person who needs a new relationship with God. As Christians seek to answer that call, we will not always know whether we have been successful, but we can trust God to work through us and others to continue the mission of Jesus. No task is more urgent in God's eyes.

Story Starter: Evangelism

Any group of church members can try this project, which is structured around two group meetings with time in between to practice evangelism. The first meeting focuses on exploring reasons for being involved in the church. To begin, each person in the group writes several statements about the most joyful and passionate aspects of their faith and their church involvement. For example, a statement could express joy about worship services that have been particularly inspiring, passion about serving others through an outreach program of the church, or thanks for a special experience of God's grace. This information is then shared through role plays presented to the whole group. Each role play involves two members of the group. One member plays the part of an unchurched friend who may be skeptical. The other has the task of sharing her or his joy with the friend. After everyone has had a chance to play both roles, the group discusses how the different roles felt. Was it difficult to share about faith with a friend who did not share your level of enthusiasm? How did you feel as the one being "evangelized"? What did you learn about evangelism from this exercise? The first meeting concludes as everyone in the group agrees to try sharing their faith with an unchurched neighbor or co-worker and to return for a second meeting in about one month. Between meetings, a designated leader can help by "checking in" with the other members, encouraging them as they share their faith beyond their church. Other members may also find it helpful to check with one another every few days.

At the second meeting, members share and reflect on their experiences. Were role plays a helpful way to practice evangelism? How did your faith-sharing experiences work out? Did anyone invite another person to visit your church? What was the response? Are you more confident in your faith as a result of your attempt to share it with a friend? Did your experience of evangelism prompt you to continue exploring ways to reach out and speak about your faith?

Questions for Discussion

1. What words do you associate with evangelism? Are the words *shepherd* or *shepherding* on your list? How has this chapter affected your concept of evangelism?

2. Have you ever been like a stray sheep in your relationship to God? If you now feel closer to God, how did the change take place? Did God use someone else to find you?

3. Do you consider yourself an evangelist? Why or why not? If not, what would prompt you to become an evangelist?

4. How does your congregation evangelize? If your church has adopted an informal or formal program of evangelism, describe it and its results. What are some of your stories?

5. Describe some of the cultures that are represented in your church and in the larger community, including your workplace and neighborhood. Can you identify possible connections between the various cultures? What approaches to evangelism would be consistent with the gospel and with the cultures of the people your church is called to reach?

6. How might you develop friendships intentionally with unchurched people at your workplace, school, or neighborhood? Can you envision yourself listening compassionately and sharing your faith?

NOTES

1. See William G. Thompson, *Matthew's Advice to a Divided Community, Mt. 17, 22–18, 35* (Rome: Biblical Institute Press, 1970), 154; Richard B. Gardner, *Matthew*, Believers Church Bible Commentary (Scottdale, Pa.: Herald Press, 1991), 277; and W. D. Davies and Dale C. Allison, Jr., *A Critical and Exegetical Commentary on the Gospel According to Saint Matthew*, vol. 2 (Edinburgh: T & T Clark, 1991), 771. According to Eduard Schweizer, *The Good News According to Matthew*, trans. David E. Green (Atlanta: John Knox Press, 1975), 368, the angelic imagery means that *God* takes the side of the little ones.

2. According to 1 Enoch 40, which probably dates from the first century B.C., there are four highest angels who stand "at the four wings of the Lord of Spirits," constantly interceding for God's people on earth. Michael is "merciful and forbearing"; Raphael is in charge of healing; Gabriel is "set over all exercise of strength"; and Phanuel is "set over all actions of repentance unto the hope of those who would inherit eternal life." 1 Enoch 54:6 states that on the day of judgment these four archangels will cast the evil hosts "into the furnace (of fire) that is burning that day, so that the Lord of Spirits may take vengeance on them on account of their oppressive

deeds which they performed as messengers of Satan, leading astray those who dwell on the earth." 1 Enoch circulated widely in the first century A.D., and it is quoted in Jude 14-15 as scripture inspired by God. The translation cited here is by E. Isaac, "I Enoch: A New Translation and Introduction," *The Old Testament Pseudepigrapha*, ed. James H. Charlesworth (Garden City, N.Y.: Doubleday, 1983), vol. 1, 7, 31-32, 38.

3. Paul J. Achtemeier, "It's the Little Things that Count (Mark 14:17-21; Luke 4:1-13; Matthew 18:10-14)," *Biblical Archeologist* 46 (1983), 30-31.

4. Douglas Hare, *Matthew* (Louisville, Ky.: John Knox, 1993), 212.

5. Davies and Allison, *Matthew*, vol. 2, 775.

6. It is more obvious in the original Greek that Matthew 18:12-13 echoes 12:11.

7. From a lecture by Herb Miller at an Evangelism Leaders Academy in Bridgewater, Virginia.

8. Names have been changed.

9. Paul McCuster, *Snapshots and Portraits* (Kansas City, Mo.: Lillenas Publishing Co., 1989). The production was organized and directed by Paula Ulrich.

10. For example, see Win Arn, "How to Find a Pastor Who Fits Your Church," *The Pastor's Church Growth Handbook*, ed. Win Arn (Pasadena, Calif.: Institute for American Church Growth, 1979), vol. 1, 8-9.

11. Blaine Minor, interview with the author, July 17, 2000.

12. Earle Fike, Jr., raised this question in a discussion on Matthew 18:10-14 at the Bethany Extension School held in Bridgewater, Virginia, in June 1997.

13. Mark Craddock, correspondence with the authors, summer 2000.

7

Direct Communication
Matthew 18:15-17

¹⁵ If another member of the church sins against you, go and point out the fault when the two of you are alone. If the member listens to you, you have regained that one. ¹⁶ But if you are not listened to, take one or two others along with you, so that every word may be confirmed by the evidence of two or three witnesses. ¹⁷ If the member refuses to listen to them, tell it to the church; and if the offender refuses to listen even to the church, let such a one be to you as a Gentile and a tax collector.

The Biblical Story

We have seen that the parable of the stray sheep (18:10-14) calls disciples to imitate Jesus' compassion in reaching out to anyone who is in danger of being lost to God's reign. Matthew 18:15-17 applies the parable to a more specific situation: What should the disciples do when one of them has sinned? As we study these verses in context, we will see that Jesus' answer calls for direct communication rather than ex-communication.

The Matthew 18:15-17 passage consists of five sentences beginning with the word "if." This pattern begins in verses 12-13 and continues in verses 18-20, suggesting that all of these verses should be interpreted in light of one another.[1] In verses 12-13, the shepherd's goal is not to punish the stray sheep, but to rescue it from danger. Likewise, the goal in verses 15-17 is not to punish, but to win back a brother or sister. The promises in verses 18-20 are also related to the preceding instructions, because the promises empower the disciples for the difficult task of correcting one another.

One significant difference between verses 15-17 and the previous sayings is that the person in need is called "your brother" (see NRSV margin) instead of "one of these little ones." We have seen that "little ones" can refer to any vulnerable person, including a child who is not yet a disciple (18:2, 6). Matthew uses "brother" or "sister" more specifically to describe the disciples' relationship to one another and to Jesus (12:49-50). Therefore, Matthew 18:15-17 is about communication between disciples, who are assumed to be members of the church (18:17).

The reference to the church in 18:17 has led some scholars to conclude that Matthew 18:15-20 does not fit well into the context of the story. Although Matthew presents these sayings as part of Jesus' earthly ministry, they seem to presuppose a time after the resurrection when the church is an established institution and when members need to be assured of Christ's presence at their gatherings.[2] The setting in the story makes better sense when we remember that Matthew's Jesus knows the future and has repeatedly predicted his own death and resurrection. Jesus is trying to prepare the disciples for their mission in the difficult time after the resurrection. Jesus' pattern has been to correct the disciples' mistakes firmly and immediately;[3] after the resurrection, however, the disciples' spiritual well-being and faithfulness in mission will depend on their ability to correct one another. The disciples' mission will be to "make disciples of all nations . . . teaching them to obey everything that I have commanded you" (28:19-20). Since correcting mistakes is an important part of teaching, Matthew 18:15-17 describes a kind of communication that the disciples will need as they disciple others. Unlike Jesus, the disciples do not know the future, and they often fail to understand Jesus' predictions; nevertheless, they have heard Jesus' promise to build the church (16:18). Further instructions about the church are quite appropriate at this point in the story.

In Matthew 18:15, Jesus instructs the disciples to get involved when they become aware that another disciple has sinned. "Sin" in Matthew's vocabulary refers to an action or attitude that falls short of fulfilling God's will as interpreted by Jesus. Since Jesus defines his brothers and sisters as "whoever does the will of my Father in heaven" (12:50), sin is a very serious matter. It threatens the disciples' relationship with God, Jesus, and one another.

The NRSV translation of 18:15 includes the phrase "against you," which places special responsibility on a disciple who feels victimized by another disciple's sin. Some important early manuscripts lack the words translated "against you," so it is difficult to decide which reading is original (see NRSV margin). The most likely explanation is that a copyist added "against you" because of the influence of "against me" in Matthew 18:21. Even if "against you" is original, it would not prevent other disciples from reaching out to the one who has sinned.[4] In Matthew's story, Jesus is concerned about any sin a disciple might commit, not only sins against another disciple. For example, in 19:13-15, Jesus confronts the disciples about their inhospitality toward children. Any sin by a disciple potentially weakens the entire community, making it less able to carry out its mission. In that sense, the sin is against all the disciples.

The visitor's task in 18:15 is not just to "point out the fault" of the one who has sinned, as stated in the NRSV. The Greek verb that is used here (*elench*) often means to "admonish" or "reprove," but its most basic meaning is to "show" or "demonstrate." The original Greek does not specify what the visitor should "point out." The visitor may need to point out how the other person has sinned, since people are often unaware of how others perceive their actions; nevertheless, there is often just as much need to point out God's grace. Members of the church who have sinned may need to be reminded that Jesus died in order to save people from their sins (1:21; 20:28; 26:28) and that forgiveness is available to all who repent. While the visitor's message will depend on the situation, the basic mission is clear: to give emergency care to a brother or sister whose spiritual health may be in danger because of sin.[5]

Matthew 18:15 is based on Leviticus 19:17, which calls for reproof as a way of loving one's neighbor. In contrast to Leviticus 19:17, however, Matthew 18:15 stresses that the initial visit should be "when the two of you are alone." This call for privacy would have been especially important for Matthew's original audience, since honor and shame were pivotal values in their culture. "Honor'" has been defined as "a claim to worth *and* the social acknowledgment of that worth."[6] Shame is the opposite, the loss of honor. In ancient Mediterranean cultures, men learned to compete for honor in every public encounter and to defend their household's honor at almost any cost.[7] Consequently, public confrontations were not the best way to seek repentance and reconciliation. The most likely result of a public confrontation would be escalating conflict as each party struggled to preserve its honor. Matthew 18:15 helps avoid that problem by calling for an initial private confrontation. Guided by that verse, a disciple will discretely pass up a chance to shame the other disciple and will focus instead on the goal of winning repentance. Matthew 18:15 also teaches against gossip and smug silence, both of which are sins rooted in pride.

The context of Matthew 18:15-17 encourages the visitor to be humble, welcoming, repentant, compassionate, prayerful, and eager to forgive—all qualities that will help to "win back" the brother or sister. These qualities imply a willingness to listen while the other person shares his or her side of the story. The visitor may have misjudged the situation, or the person being visited may show that others, including the visitor, have sinned. Hidden conflicts and long-held resentments may come out into the open. Thus, the visit may be a humbling experience for both disciples. Privacy helps protect both from unnecessary embarrassment

Since people who have sinned often disagree about who is at fault, it is important for Matthew to rule out the proud excuse that the (other) guilty party should take the initiative. Matthew 5:23-24 and 18:15 together cover all the bases. According to 5:23-24, reconciliation is even more urgent than worship, and Jesus commands his disciples to seek it immediately, regardless of who is at fault.

Matthew 18:15 describes reconciliation with a phrase that could be translated literally, "If he listens to you, you have won back your brother." In this context, listening means more than sitting still long enough to hear some words. It means heeding the visitor's call for repentance. The words "won back" are just as loaded. They imply that relationships within God's family have been restored through the patient efforts of the visitor.[8] When repentance leads to reconciliation, there is no cause for punishment, only for rejoicing that the lost has been found.

If the first visit is unsuccessful, then the next step is to try again with help from one or two others. When Jesus calls these helpers "witnesses," he is quoting Deuteronomy 19:15, which requires two witnesses as a protection from false accusations. The witnesses presumably know about the sin and are able to confirm that it happened. There is, however, an important difference between Matthew 18:16 and Deuteronomy 19:15. In Deuteronomy, the witnesses must persuade a priest or judge; in Matthew, their job is to persuade the accused. Since the goal of the visit is repentance instead of punishment, the person being visited remains in control. He or she must decide whether to accept the visitors' call for repentance.

If the call is rejected, then the next step, according to verse 17, is to bring the matter before "the church," meaning a local community of Jesus' disciples. The whole community needs to hear about the situation so they can seek God's guidance about a matter that affects them all. If they agree that one or more members have sinned, then they can add their weight to the call for repentance and reconciliation.

Throughout this process, the community's role requires compassion not only for those who have sinned but also for the victims of sin. Vulnerable people often suffer most from the sins of others. If their suffering is the result of a disciple's sin, then other disciples are called to join in confronting the offender. During the second and third steps of the disciplinary process, still other disciples join in the work of confrontation. Their solidarity with the victims of sin is consistent with God's concern for the vulnerable people whom Jesus calls "these little ones."[9] The disciples are practicing Christlike humility when they identify with vulnerable and suffering people.

It is important to note that three attempts to win back a sinful disciple are a minimum, not a maximum. The intent of verses 15-17 is that the disciples should try repeatedly and urgently to communicate the gospel with other disciples who have sinned.[10] Nothing in these verses prevents a disciple from visiting one on one several times before deciding to involve other witnesses. Steps two and three could also last a long time and require many meetings. Eventually, however, the community may decide that all its attempts to communicate the gospel have failed. The Greek verb translated "refuses to listen" in verses 16-17 suggests more than just a failure to hear the community's point of view. There is a deliberate and repeated decision not to hear. Someone who persistently refuses to listen to the community is no longer acting as a brother or sister within it. At some point, the community must sadly acknowledge what has happened.

In a first-century synagogue, treating someone as a Gentile and a tax collector probably meant "have nothing to do with the offender."[11]

In the context of Matthew's story, however, it takes on a different meaning. Jesus heals Gentiles and praises their faith (8:5-13; 15:21-28), and later he commands the disciples to make disciples of all nations (28:19). Jesus also calls a tax collector as a disciple (9:9), and he deliberately ignores the synagogue's ban on eating with tax collectors and sinners (9:10-13). In light of Jesus' example, treating someone as a Gentile and a tax collector probably means, "Treat the offender as someone who still needs to hear and accept the gospel."[12] Therefore, Matthew 18:17 does not call for "excommunication," if one defines that as "*no* communication." The church is still communicating even when it acknowledges someone's refusal to listen.[13]

If one looks for an example of excommunication in Matthew's story, Judas Iscariot may come to mind; but Judas, not Jesus, is the one who cuts off communication. Instead of excluding Judas, Jesus frankly states what is happening in their relationship (26:20-25, 47-50). After Jesus' arrest, Judas feels remorse, but he seeks forgiveness from the chief priests instead of finding it in Jesus (27:3-5). Tragically, he takes his own life.

It might be useful to imagine a different outcome to Judas's story. Imagine that Judas lives long enough to hear the news of Jesus' resurrection. The women find him just as they find each of the other guilty disciples, and they report Jesus' powerful words of restoration and forgiveness: "Do not be afraid; go and tell my brothers to go to Galilee; there they will see me" (28:10). Now Judas must decide whether he will repent, obey Jesus, and find forgiveness in Galilee. In Matthew's story, Mary Magdalene and the other Mary have the honor of being the first followers of Jesus to practice Matthew 18:15. They do so when they find the eleven male disciples who have deserted and denied Jesus. Judas, on the other hand, serves as a tragic example of what can happen when disciples fail to practice Matthew 18:15 in time.

Nothing in Matthew's story guarantees that direct communication of the gospel to sinful disciples will be a safe or simple task. Matthew 18:15-17 frankly acknowledges the risk of rejection, and there are other risks besides. Conflicts may escalate as a result of direct communication. The people trying to correct others may be blinded by their own "logs," such as arrogance or self-righteous anger (see 7:1-5). A whole community of disciples may misinterpret God's will, calling "unclean" what God considers "clean."

The risks of confrontation are real, but so are the risks of not communicating directly. Arrogance and self-righteousness are no less toxic when they are hidden in people's hearts or shared quietly in the form of gossip. Sin that is not confronted may continue in ways that are devastating for the guilty and the innocent alike, and communities may become so afraid to take a stand that they end up standing for nothing. Matthew 18:15-17 suggests that direct communication is worth the risk when it is offered with humility and compassion.

At several points in this interpretation, we have noted that Matthew 18:15-17 requires humility. That requirement should not surprise us since these verses are part of a series of elaborations on the theme that humble people are great in God's reign. Specifically, Matthew 18:15-17 helps clarify the kind of humility that Jesus models and teaches in Matthew's story. Humility, for Matthew, does not mean timidity. It means freely serving others in the name and spirit of Jesus. There are times when the best service a disciple can offer is to speak the truth in love.

Our Stories

Stories about direct communication today show that it still requires courage. Many people have difficulty determining when and how to initiate this communication. Sometimes it may even be impossible to identify the specific problem requiring attention. Levi J. Ziegler, director of Pastoral Services at the Brethren Village in Lancaster, Pennsylvania, sent the following story, which illustrates one of the ways an attempt at direct communication may fail:

> A deacon couple warmly received both my wife and me when I was a new pastor. The wife especially showered us with love and care, brought us some special dishes, and was a real friend to both of us for a period of time.
>
> All of this changed rather suddenly for no expressed reason and for no reason obvious to me. The previously warm and friendly relationship grew cold, and we did not see much of the couple. They attended worship services but never came to be greeted. I wished they would apply Matthew 18, since apparently I had offended them. The deacon body was aware of the negative feelings, but did not make a move to try to bring

about reconciliation. The cold relationship began to eat at me. I did not receive any answers through prayer, but I did begin to feel and believe that I needed to make the first move.

I arranged a visit with them. As it happened, the weather was cold the night I went to their home. They opened the door, let me in, and took my coat and hat. We sat in their living room, but this was no longer a warm place to visit. Sharing was strained and awkward. I made an effort to learn the reason for the rift between us, but the conversation was difficult and produced no results.

After some effort and perhaps a half-hour of this chilling conversation, I suggested that I ought to be leaving. The husband quickly agreed with me and rushed to get my coat and hat. I left their home that night without ever hearing from them how they had been offended. Their relationship to the church, which had also cooled by this time, remained status quo.

My conclusion was that Jesus knew what he was talking about when he said, "If you are offended, go to the one who offended you."

Unfortunately, even when they were approached directly, the people in this story were not ready to talk with Levi.

Levi sent a second story in which he again initiated direct communication. The results in this case were more positive.

The elderly lady (whom I knew fairly well) seemed to be having difficulty walking: she was stooped over and holding on to whatever she could reach. As she approached me I spoke to her about her apparent need for assistance. "Where is your cane?" I asked.

"Is my walking that bad?" she countered. I explained briefly how I saw her walking and why I asked that question. In no uncertain terms, she let me know she did not need a cane. She thanked me and walked away, telling me she would do better. She showed a coldness toward me over the ensuing weeks. Our relationship did not improve with time. I determined I needed to seek her out and right this relationship.

Before I could arrange to visit her, she called me and asked to meet. The next morning I made an appointment to visit with her. I met her in the corridor outside her apartment. Seemingly surprised to see me, she asked if I was coming to visit her. This time it was obvious that walking was difficult for her. We agreed to walk to a designated place to talk. As we walked, she held onto my arm with great dependence. Arriving at her designated place, she asked me why I came. I reminded her why I made the appointment to visit her, and assured her that I never intended to offend her. She admitted she was offended. But then she told me she forgave me, and we proceeded to talk about other matters.

It appears that this time, my visit worked. I rejoice in the way God works wonders.

This story shows that God can use our imperfect attempts at communication to heal relationships. When we visit in keeping with Matthew 18:15, we open the door for God to work.

For another variation on this theme, read this story told by a young pastor.

After officiating at my first wedding ceremony in a new pastorate, I went to the reception accompanied by my wife. There was dancing at the reception, and we decided that we would dance, too. The next day I received a call from a deacon, who said, "Some people in the church are concerned that you were dancing last night."

At first my wife and I felt upset because we see nothing wrong with a married couple dancing together. We also felt that the deacon could have been more direct in stating whether he personally had a concern. On the other hand, we were glad that he chose to communicate with us about feelings of disappointment. Once we knew about those feelings, we could decide how to respond instead of naively assuming that nothing was wrong. After talking and praying about it, we decided to stop dancing in public out of respect for the feelings of sisters and brothers who might disapprove.

This appears to be a fairly straightforward example of Matthew 18 in action. The pastor and his wife listened to the deacon's complaint and addressed it by changing their behavior. On the other hand, the story raises interesting questions about indirect communication. The deacon did not say, "I am concerned," but "Some people in the church are concerned." Apparently some church members went to the deacon first instead of the pastor. Should they have spoken to the pastor directly? Should the deacon have insisted that they communicate directly instead of passing on an indirect message? Or, if the deacon shared the concern, should he have said so? How might the pastor work to encourage direct communication under the circumstances?

Before we attempt to answer those questions, we need to discuss some basic communication skills. Afterward, we will consider how communication might have been improved in each of the three previous examples.

Communication 101

Dr. David Yoder, professor of speech pathology at the University of Wisconsin, devoted his professional life to teaching and research for the betterment of communication for people who suffered from severe communication disabilities. Yoder developed alternate communication systems for people who would never be able to use spoken language. One of his favorite sayings is, "As blood is to life, communication is to living."[14] That quote is applicable to our study of Matthew 18:15-17. The way we communicate with one another is the font of our ability to repent and to reconcile. Carolyn Schrock-Shenk makes a similar point:

> Communication lies at the heart of all interactions. It is central to all conflict because it *causes conflict* through miscommunication and misunderstanding; *it expresses conflict* verbally and nonverbally; and *it is a vehicle for conflict transformation*, positive or negative.[15]

Communication skills are central to our lives, yet it is human to resist practicing those basic skills that can enhance and enrich our relationships. The reason for this resistance is simple: communication practice is hard work!

This book is not the place for an exhaustive review of communication skills. Countless books are available for further study.[16] We also recommend studying communication in the context of the Matthew 18 Workshops offered by the Ministry of Reconciliation, a program of the On Earth Peace Assembly. The Ministry of Reconciliation is dedicated to encouraging, enabling, and empowering people to be open to the work of the Spirit in our midst for whole and healthy relationships between sisters and brothers (Matt. 18:15-22).[17] Matthew 18 Workshops can be tailored to suit the needs and interests of the participants.

Presence, listening, and speaking are all integral aspects of communication. It seems simplistic to say that you must be present to communicate; however, to be truly "present" requires a special state of being, including an attitude of respect and caring. This presence signifies a desire to understand as well as to be understood.

Listening is a commitment to suspending one's own life to pay attention to what someone else is saying. People can usually tell when someone is listening to them at a deep level. The listener is often aware of meanings and feelings that lie below the surface of what is being said. There is a creative force that comes from this kind of listening. Carolyn Schrock-Shenk describes centered listening as "tuning my energy into the heart of the other, into the center of their being."[18] Centered listening may include paraphrasing, or repeating in other words, what the speaker has said, including the feelings they have expressed.

The counterpart to centered listening is centered speaking, or speaking from the heart or center of ourselves.[19] Centered speaking often means giving information about myself and my circumstances using I-messages, messages that usually begin with the word "I." For example, "I am upset about your decision to dance at the wedding reception, because I want our church to take a clear stand against dancing." This type of speech is most effective when it is in the present tense and relates specific details rather than generalities. The critical feature is a commitment to tell only one's own story and not others' stories. If I try to speak for others, I move away from centered speaking, and I may end up blaming or misrepresenting them. They will have more reason to correct me or to become defensive. If I tell my own story, then I take responsibility for my own feelings and perceptions. I confess the truth as I see it. That truth may include my experience with Jesus and my understanding of the gospel.

Consistent, successful use of I-messages requires self-awareness, practice, and the willingness to be vulnerable; but the fruits of this discipline are worth the effort. The practice of centered speech increases the potential for successful communication during each of the encounters called for in Matthew 18:15-17. The potential for success is even greater when we combine centered listening and centered speech.

In 1999, the Union Church of the Brethren in Plymouth, Indiana, hosted a weekend workshop on successful communication. The workshop focused on Matthew 18 and included extensive Bible study and discussions of church life relative to Matthew 18. A portion of the workshop included exercises in listening and speaking. Working with another person, each workshop participant had an opportunity to use I-messages to express how they felt at the particular time. A sheet of diagrams depicting seventy different feelings was used to assist people in completing the statement "I feel _____." A number of people expressed difficulty finding the appropriate word to reflect their feeling, but these drawings provided them with the vocabulary they needed. In addition to the seventy examples, the drawings stimulated other feeling words not included on the worksheet. This fun, revealing exercise provided good I-message practice in a nonthreatening environment.

The workshop leaders also introduced and modeled paraphrasing as a way to listen actively. Several small-group exercises gave everyone the opportunity to focus on a speaker and restate the facts and feelings they heard in a brief phrase or sentence. After listeners completed a paraphrase, the other participants described how it sounded. For many this painstaking work required unusual effort. They reported they paid closer attention and heard more details. The exercises were illuminating; people who had believed they were good listeners, were surprised to learn how much better they could become. Practicing good listening and speaking skills pays dividends!

Clyde Carter reported this experience from a Matthew 18 Workshop he led:

> It was an "overnight" workshop dealing with scripture and communication. During a series of communication exercises, the dozen participants worked together in pairs. I always invite any husbands and wives present to team up for these exercises. After three multi-hour sessions, we had a verbal evaluation, which turned into a tear-jerker. A husband and wife were sitting at the far end of a table from me when he began to speak. "For decades my wife has been telling me I am not listening to her," he began. Everyone was dead silent as he shifted his body position toward his dear wife. He told her and us that as result of this Matthew 18 workshop he understood what she was saying. As tears rolled

down several cheeks, he continued to look at his wife and say, "I
understand now. I will listen. I will change"— and the entire
workshop group gave one another the gift of silence as we
thanked God.[20]

Mastering the skills of centered listening and speaking is a lifelong
process. We can learn from every direct communication experience.
Both journaling and discussing our experiences with others can provide insights and new ways to respond in subsequent situations. With
experience and prayer, we can be more fully present to each other, and
we can be centered listeners and speakers.

Our Stories Revisited

Now let us revisit the first three stories briefly to see how communication might have become more direct and centered. Levi Ziegler was
especially attentive and direct during his second conversation with the
lady who had difficulty walking. He shared his observations and his
feelings about wanting to communicate with her. He stated clearly
that he did not wish to offend her. The lady heard him and accepted
his apology.

Levi's visit with the couple, however, produced no clarity about the
topic. He was sure there was a breach in their relationship, but his
attempts to identify the problem were unsuccessful. Since we do not
know the specific conversation that occurred, we do not know what
type of I-messages they expressed or how they heard one another. Perhaps the "cold" setting did not allow anyone to express feelings about
the situation. As Levi left the parishioners' home, he might have said,
"I have been troubled by the change I have sensed in our relationship.
I do not feel that I understand much more than when I came here tonight. I would like another opportunity to speak about this with you. I
am going to think and pray about this visit. How would you feel about
doing the same thing? Could I call you about this in one week? I would
appreciate hearing from you any time you wish to call me. Thank you
for seeing me tonight." With such an effort, Levi would have expressed
himself clearly and opened the door to additional opportunities for direct communication.

The story about dancing demonstrates that a person being confronted
about a perceived sin remains in control because he or she can decide

how to respond. Although the pastor and his wife decided to stop dancing in public, they could have discounted the deacon's comments since they saw nothing wrong with a married couple dancing. That decision could have prompted additional discussions. Perhaps a fuller articulation of the pastor's feelings would have changed the attitudes of the people who were criticizing him. Meanwhile, another possibility would have been to paraphrase the deacon's message and ask for more information. For example, the pastor could have replied, "It sounds like my decision to dance at the reception last night is a problem for some members of the church. How do you personally feel about my decision?"

We have already raised questions about the deacon's decision to speak for others in this situation. Although some might argue that speaking for others is an occupational hazard for deacons, we believe it is usually better to insist on direct communication. We recognize that pastors are in positions of power and that approaching them may be difficult for some members. Because of this difficulty, some congregations have pastoral relations committees that can decide either to pass concerns on to the pastor or to insist that they be shared directly. The pastor also should clarify with the congregation what she or he expects in communication with them. In general, we believe that pastors, deacons, and other church leaders are responsible for teaching and modeling direct communication. In most cases, this will mean going in private to the person with whom one has a complaint—and insisting that others do the same.

On the other hand, there are situations in which we would not recommend that someone visit an offender alone. For example, a private confrontation could be far too dangerous for someone who is a victim of domestic violence; we would encourage her or him to seek outside help immediately. Often in cases of domestic violence, there have already been many private confrontations. The second or third stages described in Matthew 18:16-17 are long overdue.

Even though there are situations where direct communication is not advisable, there are many more where it is difficult but necessary. In response to our request for stories about Matthew 18, several pastors reported dismay at how infrequently they had observed direct communication. Although these pastors frequently heard complaints of one brother or sister against another, their attempts to encourage people to speak directly to one another were unsuccessful. A typical response to

Story Starter: I-Messages

Practice I-messages. First review the description of I-messages in this chapter. Then pay close attention to your communication in at least one conversation with someone close to you. Choose a conversation in which you feel a need to share concerns and feelings that are important to you. As you reflect on the conversation afterward, do you feel you were able to share in clear and helpful ways? Did you attempt to use I-messages? If so, how were they received? Was your use of I-messages consistent with your body language, gestures, and intonation?

Next, pay attention to your behavior in a second conversation in which you intentionally use more I-messages. Did the number of such messages increase? Was the context and emotional content of your conversation enhanced by your use of I-messages? Which conversation do you believe was more successful? Did your conversation partner notice your use of I-messages? How did she or he perceive the conversations? Would you like I-messages to become more of a habit as you communicate one on one with others?

You may find it helpful to record these conversations so that you can compare your memory with what was actually said. Of course, you will need permission, and there is some danger that a tape recorder will inhibit the conversation. On the other hand, a recording may help you to notice I-messages that you were unaware of at the time.

As a second part of this exercise, be aware of your conversation with others in a group, such as at a church committee meeting. Again, be alert for your use of I-messages, and consider asking permission to record the meeting. As you review the tape or your memories of the meeting, compare your communication style there with your style away from the church. (By communication style we mean tone of voice, choice of words, body language, etc.) Do the different contexts demand different communication styles? Are I-messages as useful in a group setting as in one-on-one conversation?

You may also have an opportunity to encourage the rest of the committee to use I-messages. As a group project, the committee could decide to record and review a meeting in which the members try to use more I-messages. Afterward, ask members to evaluate their communication at that meeting. Do they believe the work of the committee was enhanced by the use of I-messages? What other strategies might help to improve communication among members?

pastoral suggestions for direct communication was, "Oh, I don't think I could do that. You know how I can't stand conflict."

Another pastor recounted an experience that occurred at the conclusion of a Matthew 18 Workshop hosted by the church. A member came to the pastor and said he felt called to discuss a problem with another member. The workshop had touched this man and prompted him to follow through with direct communication. We need to practice this type of response more frequently in the church.

Questions for Discussion

1. Recall two conversations that you have had recently, one that was pleasant and one that was difficult or uncomfortable for some reason. While considering each of the key elements of communication (speaking, listening, and the message), identify aspects of each conversation that were positive and aspects that were more challenging. What factors made the one conversation difficult or uncomfortable? What would you do differently if you could repeat the conversations?

2. According to Carolyn Schrock-Shenk, "Communication is central to all conflict. Communication causes conflict through miscommunication and misunderstanding; it expresses conflict verbally and nonverbally; and it is a vehicle for conflict transformation, positive or negative." What stories in your life does this quotation bring to mind?

3. Direct communication with people you believe have sinned requires risk. What risks were mentioned in this chapter, and what risks can you add from your personal experience? What are the risks of *not* communicating directly? Give specific examples.

4. The authors emphasize the importance of privacy in the initial visit with someone who may have sinned. What benefits of privacy have you experienced in direct communication with someone? Are there any drawbacks?

5. Although a private visit is sometimes too dangerous, more often it is difficult and necessary. Do you agree? Name situations when a private visit would fit each of these categories: (a) too dangerous, (b) difficult but necessary, (c) unnecessary. How do you decide which is which?

6. Discuss the results of successful direct communication—the three R's: repentance, reconciliation, and rejoicing. Why is punishment not an expected result?

7. Do you agree that the person being visited according to Matthew 18:15 remains in control because he or she decides whether to accept the visitors' call for repentance? How might issues of control or power affect the outcome of such visits?

8. These verses often elicit negative responses from people who have experienced or heard stories about "the ban" or excommunication. Share these stories and reflect on how you interpret them after studying this chapter. Have any of your assumptions or conclusions changed?

9. Consider Judas as an example of excommunication. The chapter states that Judas repeatedly cut off communication. Did this interpretation of Judas's story enhance your understanding of Matthew 18:15?

NOTES

1.William G. Thompson, *Matthew's Advice to a Divided Community, Mt. 17, 22–18, 35* (Rome: Biblical Institute Press, 1970), 176.

2. For example, see Jack Dean Kingsbury, *Matthew as Story*, 2nd ed. (Philadelphia: Fortress Press, 1988), 109.

3. For example, compare Matthew 6:25-34 with 8:23-27; 10:8 with 17:14-20; and 18:5 with 19:13-15.

4. Richard B. Gardner, *Matthew*, Believers Church Bible Commentary (Scottdale, Pa.: Herald Press, 1991), 281; Estella B. Horning, "The Rule of Christ: An Exposition of Matthew 18:15-20," *Brethren Life and Thought* 38 (1993), 69-78.

5. Marlin Jeschke, *Discipling in the Church: Recovering a Ministry of the Gospel*, 3rd ed. (Scottdale, Pa.: Herald Press, 1988), 17.

6. Bruce J. Malina, *The New Testament World: Insights from Cultural Anthropology* (Louisville, Ky.: John Knox Press, 1993), 28 (emphasis original).

7. Malina, *New Testament World*, 42-47; Jerome H. Neyrey, *Honor and Shame in the Gospel of Matthew* (Louisville, Ky.: Westminster/John Knox Press, 1998), 29-32.

8. David Daube, "*Kerdain* as a Missionary Term," *Harvard Theological Review* 40 (1947), 109-20.

9. Elaine Ramshaw, "Power and Forgiveness in Matthew 18," *Word and World* 18 (1998), 403.

10. Thompson, *Advice*, 186.

11. Dennis C. Duling, "Matthew 18:15-17: Conflict, Confrontation, and Conflict Resolution in a 'Fictive Kin' Association," in *SBL 1998 Seminar Papers Part One* (Atlanta: Scholars Press,

1998), 253-95; Göran Forkman, *The Limits of Religious Community: Expulsion from the Religious Community Within the Qumran Sect, Within Rabbinic Judaism, and Within Primitive Christianity* (Lund: C. W. K. Gleerup, 1972), 92-105; and John R. Donahue, "Tax Collectors and Sinners: An Attempt at Identification," *Catholic Biblical Quarterly* 33 (1971), 46.

12. Thompson, *Advice*, 185; Donald Senior, *Invitation to Matthew: A Commentary on the Gospel of Matthew with Complete Text from the Jerusalem Bible* (Garden City, N.Y.: Image Books, 1977), 182; George T. Montague, *Companion God: A Cross-Cultural Commentary on the Gospel of Matthew* (New York: Paulist Press, 1989), 201.

13. According to Thompson (*Advice*, 185), the singular pronoun "to you" in 18:17 suggests that treating someone as a Gentile and a tax collector "is a matter of personal attitude and conduct" rather than a collective action by the whole community. This argument sounds correct until one accounts for the next three verses (18:18-20), which use plural pronouns and emphasize the need for agreement by the disciples who have gathered as the church. It would violate this principle of agreement if only one disciple were to treat the unrepentant offender as "a Gentile and a tax collector."

14. David E. Yoder, lecture presented at the School of Arts and Sciences, Indiana University-Purdue University, Fort Wayne, Indiana, March 23, 1984.

15. Carolyn Schrock-Shenk, *Mediation and Facilitation Training Manual: Foundations and Skills for Constructive Conflict Transformation*, 3rd ed., eds. Jim Stutzman and Carolyn Schrock-Shenk (Akron, Pa.: Mennonite Conciliation Service, 1995), 108.

16. For further information, see Carol Mayhall, *Words that Hurt, Words that Heal* (Colorado Springs: NavPress, 1989); Robert Gross, *Mediating Interpersonal Conflict* (North Manchester, Ind.: Education for Conflict Resolution, Inc., 1997); Barbara Date, *Understanding, Healing and Bridgebuilding: Listening Together: The Date Discernment Circle* (Winnipeg: Menno Simons College; University of Winnipeg, 1996), and *Tools for Harmony Within Diversity: Skills for Daily Interpersonal Peacemaking "The Foreign Language of Caring"* (Winnipeg: Menno Simons College; University of Winnipeg, 1998); Jim Stutzman and Carolyn Schrock-Shenk, eds., *Mediation and Facilitation Training Manual, Foundations and Skills for Constructive Conflict Transformation* (Akron, Pa.: Mennonite Conciliation Service, 1995); Michael P. Nichols, *The Lost Art of Listening: How Learning to Listen Can Improve Relationships* (New York: The Guilford Press, 1995); Patricia Loring, *Listening Spirituality: Personal Spiritual Practices Among Friends* (Washington, D.C.: Openings Press, 1997); Roger Fisher and William Ury, *Getting to Yes: Negotiating Agreement Without Giving In* (New York: Penguin Books, 1991); William Ury, *Getting Past No: Negotiating with Difficult People* (New York: Bantam Books, 1991).

17. From a Ministry of Reconciliation membership brochure.

18. Schrock-Shenk, *Training Manual*, 110.

19. Ronald Kraybill, *Mediation and Facilitation Training Manual: Foundations and Skills for Constructive Conflict Transformation*, 3rd ed., eds. Jim Stutzman and Carolyn Schrock-Shenk (Akron, Pa.: Mennonite Conciliation Service, 1995), 109.

20. Clyde Carter, e-mail communication with Dan Ulrich, December 4, 2001.

8

Shared Authority
Matthew 18:18-20

¹⁸ Truly I tell you, whatever you bind on earth will be bound in heaven, and whatever you loose on earth will be loosed in heaven. ¹⁹ Again, truly I tell you, if two of you agree on earth about anything you ask, it will be done for you by my Father in heaven. ²⁰ For where two or three are gathered in my name, I am there among them.

The Biblical Story

In Matthew 18:15-17, Jesus encourages the disciples to speak with one another directly and repeatedly (if necessary) when one of them has sinned. If an offender refuses to heed private admonitions, the entire community of disciples may become involved in hearing about the situation and calling for repentance. These bold instructions raise questions about the nature and extent of the disciples' authority. For example, who decides what is a sin and when has a sinner repented? Such questions are on the agenda as Matthew expands the series of conditional sentences that began in verses 12-13 and 15-17. Three conditional promises in verses 18-20 complement the commands of verses 15-17. These promises empower the disciples in their communication with one another and with God.

The first promise relates very closely to the disciplinary situation described in verses 15-17. "Bind" and "loose" are technical terms for a rabbi's authority to teach and discipline the members of a synagogue. In some rabbinic writings, these terms refer to decisions about whether a particular action is acceptable under the law. To "bind" is to forbid an action, while to "loose" is to permit it. The same words can be used for forgiving or not forgiving sins (compare John 20:23). Either of these meanings fits the context of Matthew 18:18, and it is possible that Jesus promises both kinds of authority to the disciples.[1] We have already seen that for Matthew teaching and discipline go hand in hand.

When someone reports an alleged sin to the community in keeping with 18:17, several decisions are possible. The disciples could decide either that the behavior in question was not a sin or that the offender had repented and returned to the community as a brother or sister. In either case, the disciples would be exercising their power to "loose." On the other hand, the disciples could determine that one of them had sinned *and* had rejected the community's calls for repentance. In that case, they would be deciding to "bind."

Matthew's Jesus models each of these forms of binding and loosing. He binds swearing (5:33-37) and in-kind retaliation (5:38-42), but looses gleaning and healing on the sabbath (12:1-14). He looses the sins of a paralyzed man (9:2-8), but apparently binds the Pharisees' blasphemy against the Holy Spirit (12:31-32). Jesus interprets and fulfills God's will with authority (7:28-29; 28:18), and it is his prerogative to share that authority with the disciples.[2]

The plural pronouns in verse 18 suggest that the disciples will exercise this authority as a community. Earlier in the story, Jesus makes the same promise to Peter, using singular pronouns (16:19). Peter is probably functioning as a representative of the other disciples even there,[3] but after 18:18 there can be no doubt that Jesus intends for all the disciples to share the authority to bind and to loose. Shared authority means that disciples should act differently from a rabbi, who might rule over a synagogue alone. Jesus makes this difference explicit in Matthew 23:6-8: "[The Pharisees] love to have the place of honor at banquets and the best seats in the synagogues, and to be greeted with respect in the marketplaces, and to have people call them rabbi. But you are not to be called rabbi, for you have one teacher, and you are all students." Matthew's understanding of humility does not allow for either individualism or authoritarianism. His story calls instead for the discernment of God's will in community.

The meaning of Jesus' promise depends on how one interprets the Greek grammar of verse 18.[4] Matthew uses the future perfect tense to describe God's actions in heaven. The verse could be translated literally: "Whatever you bind on earth *will have been* bound in heaven, and whatever you loose on earth *will have been* loosed in heaven." The difference between this translation and the NRSV (quoted above) is significant. According to the NRSV, Jesus promises that God will uphold the disciples' decisions. According to the alternate translation, Jesus promises that the disciples will correctly discern what God has already decided. The NRSV is probably correct here. Greek writers sometimes used the future perfect tense where we would use the simple future. In addition, "will be loosed" is consistent with verse 19, which clearly speaks of God responding to an agreement by the disciples. Jesus evidently shares real authority with the disciples, allowing them to participate in shaping God's decisions.

Even if we adopt the NRSV translation, however, we need to remember Matthew's heavy emphasis on obedience to God's will. Jesus defines God's family as "whoever does the will of my Father in heaven" (12:50). He teaches the disciples to pray "Your will be done" (6:10), and he models submission to God's will in his prayer at Gethsemane (26:39). When we read Matthew 18:18 in that context, it is clear that Jesus is not inviting the disciples to manipulate God. The assumption behind Jesus' promise is that the disciples will try to discern and do whatever God wants.

Unfortunately, the disciples' record in that regard is not encouraging. After receiving Jesus' initial promise of the power to bind and to loose in 16:19, Peter proceeds to rebuke Jesus for predicting suffering and death in Jerusalem (16:22-23); he offers to build three booths so that Jesus, Moses, and Elijah can stay on the Mount of Transfiguration (17:4); and he answers thoughtlessly that Jesus pays the temple tax (17:25). These are not sterling examples of discernment, but Jesus is thinking about the future, not the past, when he renews the promise in 18:18. Jesus envisions a humbled Peter, someone who has learned from the experiences of Passover week and who will finally be ready to listen before he speaks. Jesus also expects to be present in spirit wherever the disciples gather in his name (18:20). He will help to guide their collective decisions.

Decisions will be necessary, of course, because new situations will inevitably raise new questions about God's will. Some of the hardest questions in Matthew's time had to do with the terms under which Gentiles could join the church. Should they be required to uphold the law of Moses including circumcision, or was faith in Christ sufficient? Acts 15 may give the impression that the apostles settled this issue easily at a conference in Jerusalem, but Paul's letter to the Galatians gives a different perspective. Paul was furious that missionaries who required circumcision were preaching "a different gospel" to his converts in Galatia (Gal. 1:6). He even wished that the missionaries' knife would slip so they would castrate themselves (Gal. 5:12)! If Acts 15 and Galatians 2 describe the same meeting, we have clear evidence that the conflict over circumcision was not settled there. Another tough issue was whether Christians could eat meat that had been sacrificed to idols, a practice forbidden in Acts 15:20 but approved by Paul so long as no one's conscience was offended (1 Cor. 8–10). Some Christians *were* offended even in the late first century, as Revelation 2:20 attests: "You tolerate that woman Jezebel, who calls herself a prophet and is teaching and beguiling my servants to practice fornication and to eat food sacrificed to idols."

It is not always easy to discern Matthew's perspective on these issues. He included sayings that require strict obedience to the law of Moses (5:17-20), but he also reported that Jesus reinterpreted the law according to its original intention, relaxing it in some cases and tightening it in others. In Matthew, Jesus seems as liberal about food laws as he is about the sabbath (15:1-20). There is at least one point where Paul and Matthew clearly agree: Love of God and neighbor is the essence of the law (Matt. 22:34-40; Rom. 13:8-10). This principle helps explain Jesus' various reinterpretations of the law. The bottom line for Matthew was that disciples must obey the law of Moses *as interpreted by Jesus* (28:20). Matthew understood that the risen Jesus would continue to guide the disciples as new questions arose, but agreeing about specific issues was apparently as difficult for the early church as it is today.

That difficulty is part of the background for the next promise, which affirms that God will grant any request agreed upon by two or more disciples. The beginning of verse 19 ("Again, truly I tell you") suggests that this promise is closely related to the first. Probably the authority to bind and to loose is a specific way to apply the power of united prayer. A call for united prayer is especially relevant for a disciplinary situation where an agreement would bring reconciliation. Since only two disciples must agree, the promise can apply at any stage of the disciplinary process described in verses 15-17. If the process leads to an agreement, the disciples involved can claim the authority to loose sin by means of their united prayer.

Meanwhile, verse 19 could apply not only to disciplinary situations but also to any prayer on which two disciples agree. Matthew encourages simple prayers for basic needs, and he emphasizes God's desire to listen and respond in love (6:5-6; 7:7-11). The promise "It will be done for you by my Father in heaven" (18:19) echoes the Lord's Prayer, which is a model for united prayer by the disciples (6:9-13). The Lord's Prayer uses plural pronouns like "our," "us," and "we," so it is a community prayer even when someone says it alone. It allows room for day-to-day concerns but not for selfish individualism: "Give us this day our daily bread" could presumably include all of humanity.[5] The Lord's Prayer also highlights the urgency of mutual forgiveness, and it models Jesus' expectation that the disciples will pray according to God's will.

A troubling aspect of Matthew 18:19 is that Jesus' promise does not always seem true. Many prayers remain unanswered even though faithful disciples wholeheartedly agree to them. Matthew might respond by pointing out that God has not yet fully answered the Lord's Prayer. Like many Jews and Christians of his day, Matthew expected God's end-time reign of peace and justice to enter the world like a painful birth (24:8). There would be a time of great suffering followed by a glorious intervention by God. The will of God, violated for so long, would finally be done "on earth as it is in heaven." For Matthew, the Lord's Prayer was a call for the fulfillment of God's promised end-time reign. In spite of that prayer, however, Matthew lived in a time of terror. In A.D. 66–70, Roman armies devastated all of Palestine and then surrounded Jerusalem for three years until they had starved it into submission. Eventually the city and its temple were destroyed. Many Christians and Jews concluded that God must intervene immediately, but not Matthew. The answer he heard from Jesus could be summarized, Watch and wait! I will return with power to establish God's end-time reign of justice and peace, but you do not know when, so be ready *and* patient (24:1–25:13).

The wait has proven much longer than Matthew could have guessed, but the essential relationship between prayer and patience remains the same. Matthew 18:19 gives no deadline for God to respond. God answers many prayers immediately and some of them miraculously. If we have eyes to see, we rejoice at the evidence of God's power and love. For other prayers, however, God's answer is, "Be patient." Jesus' resurrection is a reminder that God's yes may come after death. In some cases, it will not come until God finally says yes to the Lord's Prayer.

Matthew's patience in waiting for Jesus' visible return is due partly to his faith in Jesus' ongoing spiritual presence. Jesus is " 'Emmanuel,' which means, 'God is with us' " (1:23). Likewise, the final words of Matthew's story are, "I am with you always, to the end of the age" (28:20). Thus, the final promise in Matthew 18:18-20 resonates with key affirmations at the beginning and end of the story: Jesus will be present whenever two or three people gather in his name.

Verse 20 makes it clear that Jesus' presence is the basis for the earlier promises in this section. The word "for" suggests that God will answer the disciples' prayers *because* Jesus is present in their midst. The phrase, "gathered in my name" makes a similar point. As we observed in connection with Matthew 18:5, "in my name" can indicate either the reason for an action or the power behind it. Both meanings are possible here, but the context puts more emphasis on power. Jesus' presence will empower the disciples as they attempt to discern God's will and unite in prayer.

All of this means that the disciples' authority is a gift from Jesus. It does not depend on their own wisdom, nor on their number, gender, age, seniority, or social status. The ancient rule requiring ten adult males to form a synagogue does not apply.[6] For the same reason, Matthew does not envision a church hierarchy. The risen Jesus himself will govern the small house churches that missionaries will start as they travel from city to city. Any two or three disciples can "be the church," which exists wherever people have gathered around Jesus.

Matthew's emphasis on shared authority and small numbers contributes to the overall theme of Matthew 18, which is that humble people are great in God's reign. We have already observed God's concern for "one such child" (18:5), "one of these little ones" (18:6, 10, 14), and one sheep (18:12). Here we see the importance of only two or three disciples. A tiny congregation that relies on Jesus can wield enormous power.

The repetition of "among them" in 18:2 and 18:20 suggests another connection to the theme of humility. In 18:2, Jesus identifies himself with a lowly child who is standing among the disciples; in 18:20 he uses the same phrase to promise that he will be among them. The repetition certainly serves as a reminder of Jesus' humility. It may also hint that Jesus will be present in the form of a "little one." As disciples attempt to discern God's will collectively, they will be wise to heed voices that too often are ignored—the voices of children and other lowly people.

Although authority and humility may seem incompatible, Matthew's story shows that they belong together. Jesus wields "all authority in heaven and on earth" (28:18), but he is humble in that he uses his authority to serve others (20:28). Matthew 18 encourages the disciples to combine authority and humility in the same way.

In our opinion, Jesus especially models humility in his willingness to attend so many meetings, including the tedious ones where people try to work out their differences. As we consider the context of Matthew 18, it is worth asking why Jesus would promise to be present with the disciples if his conflict with them is so sharp. Just before Matthew 18, he complains bitterly about their insufficient faith: "You faithless and perverse generation, how much longer must I put up with you?" (17:17). Jesus' frustration with the disciples makes the promise in 18:20 even more significant. He could decide to give up on them, but he promises to keep trying, like the diligent shepherd in the parable. Jesus will come not because the disciples deserve him, but because they need him. He fulfills God's will at every turn. He will go to Jerusalem in order to confront the religious leaders at the seat of their power, and he will be spiritually present at every meeting the disciples hold in his name.

Our Stories

Matthew's emphasis on shared authority is especially relevant for Christians today who struggle to agree. We begin this section with three stories about congregations that struggled patiently until they found a way forward together. We end with a review of the Church of the Brethren's most recent statement about abortion.

The first story comes from Allen Hansell, who at the time was pastor of the Wilmington (Delaware) Church of the Brethren:

> In 1973, the church was caught in a dilemma. The church owned a house next door that was being used as a community center. It was in terrible condition. A group of members wanted to tear it down and make space for a badly needed parking lot. Another group wanted to renovate it and turn it into a parsonage for the pastoral family. At the time, the church was giving me and my family a housing allowance, and we were living in rental property. Both groups wanted me to state my position, each hoping that I would take up its cause. I felt it was a church decision, and I stated that I would be happy to live with either choice.
>
> The church board, after a great deal of struggle, recommended to the council meeting that the house be renovated and turned into a parsonage. The issue was hotly debated in the council meeting, and the board's recommendation passed by a one-vote majority.
>
> The congregational moderator, Dr. Caleb Bucher, asked the congregation for a few minutes to confer with me before closing the meeting. We agreed that the vote was too close for the congregation to move forward. So we suggested that the members go home and, in the spirit of Matthew 18, talk to each other and pray about the matter and return the following Sunday ready to reopen the issue.
>
> We gathered on the following Sunday. After another heated debate, the board's recommendation was rejected, and someone moved that the house be torn down and turned into a parking lot. That vote went the other way by a three-vote majority. Caleb Bucher and I conferred on next steps. Again, we felt that the church was too divided to move forward. So, we recommended that the congregation table the matter for three months. During

that time, we urged the members to pray and talk to each other about their different opinions in an effort to find a consensus. The congregation voted to accept our recommendation.

Three months later, we convened the council meeting to vote on the board's original recommendation to renovate the house and make it a parsonage. There was very little discussion. It was uncanny. Someone called for a vote, and support for the board's recommendation was nearly unanimous. There were less than a half dozen "no" votes.

That was remarkable in itself; but a far more remarkable thing happened. One of the leading persons in the opposition group volunteered to chair a renovation committee, and he challenged people on both sides of the issue to form a committee to work with him. We very quickly formed a committee.

Those folks worked together for nearly a year, with lots of help from other volunteers in the church, to renew that old property. They also added a large family room, two bedrooms, a powder room, and a laundry room. The work was done totally by the members and everything was completely paid for when we moved into the newly renovated house in 1974. We lived there until I went to a new pastorate in 1985. The parsonage is being used by the current pastoral family.

Matthew 18 encourages conversation and a process that leads hopefully to win-win situations.[7]

Allen Hansell's story reflects a traditional method of sharing authority in Church of the Brethren congregations. Important decisions are made through a vote of the congregational business meeting (also called the "council meeting"), which includes all members of the congregation. An elected church board (sometimes called a "leadership team") makes recommendations to the congregational business meeting and sees that the congregation's decisions are carried out. The pastor gives leadership but does not control the decisions. As pastor, Allen Hansell was careful not to take sides in a decision where he could be perceived as acting in his own interest. He did, however, exercise strong leadership in regard to the decision-making process.

A more recent story comes from Irvin Heishman, who co-pastors the Harrisburg First Church of the Brethren along with his wife, Nancy Sollenberger Heishman. With their leadership, the congregation has developed an extensive social ministry, including a program that responds to the housing needs of disadvantaged families. *Messenger* (a denominational magazine) has featured this congregation as a model of effective urban ministry.[8] Here Irvin describes the first serious conflict experienced by the congregation in more than forty years:

A Spanish-speaking congregation outgrew the living room where they started, and they came to see if they could share space with us. We have a long history of doing that so we said yes, and over the next year a really positive relationship developed between us. The Olivencias, who pastor the Spanish-speaking group, came to us one Sunday and asked if they could be members of First Church. And we said, "Does that mean the two of you or the whole fellowship?" And they said, "The whole fellowship." So we began a process of discernment. It was a dating relationship in a way, and it went very well. They ended up becoming part of the congregation. The English group continued to meet in the morning for Sunday school and worship, and the Spanish group worshiped in the afternoons.

The first time I realized there was some trouble brewing about all of that was when we had our first joint love feast. We did the service bilingually, and it was a high moment for a lot of people in the church, but afterward there was criticism that the translation disrupted the service and made it longer. It caught us off guard as leaders, but we assumed that it was a minority of people, and that they would adjust. But that was the beginning of our awareness that unity between Spanish and English speakers wasn't automatic and that there was going to be a lot of work involved in bringing us together.

To complicate matters even more, we were having success in welcoming more African-Americans into our morning worship service. This was fulfilling our vision statement which called for our congregation to become a multicultural church. We knew that this vision would require many changes, including changes in worship. One new African-American visitor said, "I don't know why God wants me in this church. I feel like I have to sit on my hands during worship." Finally she decided that God was teaching her to "be still and know that I am God." She was very gracious, but we knew we couldn't expect everyone to make that kind of adjustment. We knew it wasn't fair to say, "We want to be multicultural but everybody has to come and do things the way we have always done it." So we began experimenting with more diversity in style in our worship services. An African-American woman who was a wonderful soloist in the black gospel style began attending. We invited her to sing with our choir. Unfortunately, her flamboyant personality rubbed some members the wrong way. We began to feel resistance to making too much change in worship, so it was hard to move toward being truly multicultural. My wife wondered aloud in a sermon about how much we can stretch, using the image of a rubber band, which if stretched too much will break. We tested those limits with blended worship, and finally we came to the conclusion that there was not enough elasticity in our existing worship service to move toward a multicultural blend.

The idea of launching a new multicultural worship service began to look like a good solution. Yet, at the same time, there were strong fears that this direction would break our faith community apart. A year ago a decision was made to go ahead and start a new service, but a financial bind that year didn't give us the resources to go ahead. And there wasn't a real sense of unity around that decision, so we continued to struggle with the issues. At the same time, our Spanish pastor suffered a serious health crisis, which was a major setback in our Spanish ministry. I can honestly say that by the beginning of 2001 the congregation was in crisis. The emotional intensity of the discernment process grew as underlying issues of racism and fear of losing people in proposed changes were identified.

The key to a successful resolution came as our leadership team recognized that they needed to listen carefully to the congregation and then struggle with the issues until they arrived at a consensus among themselves. Then they hoped to help the congregation become involved in fine-tuning and owning the direction they would propose. The leadership team began scheduling a series of extra congregational and leadership team meetings. They agonized together over what they felt God was calling the congregation to do. It was hard for them because the leadership team this year just happened to be more heavily weighted with more tradition-minded, older members, the ones who were the least interested in change. There were some very intense meetings where we were heatedly honest with one another. We dealt with issues of racism and the need for change. It was an amazing process as they struggled together, prayed, cleared the air, confessed their fears, and then came back together again and again. There was an incredible love and a commitment that emerged. Over six or seven months of work together, a consensus started to emerge among the leaders. Eventually it became a unanimous consensus among the team, which was a remarkable achievement, because there was much reluctance initially to boldly face these issues.

After the leadership team reached a consensus, they worked very carefully in sharing that general direction with the congregation. They first consulted with the Spanish members of the church because the new direction would most directly affect them. We were asking them to prayerfully consider joining us in launching a new bilingual, multicultural worship service. Their service would be folded into the new one. We assured them that if they decided this did not feel like the direction God was calling them, we would affirm that and go back to the drawing board with them in order to find a new solution. They took about a month to pray and reflect on the proposal. They raised a lot of excellent questions that informed the final recommendation. They also found many benefits for them in the proposal and eagerly affirmed it.

The leaders next took the proposal to the English speaking members of the church. They carefully shared the reasons for the general direction proposed and asked for input about details wherever possible. The plan was to move the traditional English worship service to an earlier hour. The earlier hour of 9:00 was chosen following a survey of the congregation. This was to be followed by the Sunday school hour. Then the new bilingual worship service would be held at 11:00 a.m., because it seemed unlikely that many inner-city residents would come out for an early service.

One thing I like about the new schedule is that it puts the Sunday school in between. The Sunday school will be a place where the sense of community across the worship services can be built. The Spanish group had not had the benefit of a Sunday school, so they were excited about that part of the plan and felt it would bring us together.

In worship, the leadership team presented a series of Moments of Mission, sharing from their hearts about the new proposal.

One gave a powerful presentation. He said, "I have never in all my forty-five years of church leadership gone through an issue where we came so close to sweating blood over what we needed to be doing." He said he realized when we went into this process that there were no easy answers and no perfect solution. But he said that the proposal arrived at was worth giving our best effort. He urged the congregation to give the proposal prayerful consideration.

The other thing that was happening during this time was that a group of people started gathering on Wednesday nights to pray for the church. That was also when the Spanish group had their Bible study, so they all began praying together. We were undergirded with prayer through this whole process. The council meeting was very well attended. The leadership team asked for a two-thirds vote and used a paper ballot because they didn't want anybody to feel intimidated. The vote for the proposal was eighty-two percent, which wasn't a total consensus; but, given the complexity of the decision and its far-reaching ramifications, it was quite significant.[9]

Both of these stories are significant, not because they resulted in perfect answers, but because each congregation worked patiently and prayerfully toward an answer that was "worth the best efforts" of everyone involved. In both stories, the process for making a decision was probably at least as important as the outcome. Each congregation benefitted from strong servant-oriented leaders who helped people move through conflict in a constructive way. Each congregation continued to pray and wrestle with the issues until it was clear that a consensus (or near consensus) had emerged.

Our next story also reflects patient, prayerful consensus-building by a congregation with strong leadership. In this case, however, the congregation had to decide how much to trust the repentance of a member who had sinned.

Martha (not her real name) was a Sunday school teacher and an active member of the Marion Church of the Brethren when she was convicted of child molestation and sentenced to twelve years in prison. None of the children she molested were connected with the congregation. The current pastor, who began after the conviction, learned to know Martha by visiting her in prison. He knew she wanted to return to her church. He also visited Martha's husband, who started coming to church more frequently as a result.

Approximately eighteen months before Martha's expected release, the pastor initiated discussion with the congregation about how best to respond. Reactions varied from skeptical and unsure ("Does she really want to return to our church?") to vehemently negative ("If she comes back, I leave!") to strongly positive ("Of course she comes back here!").

A diverse, seven-member committee was formed a few months later to explore the issues. One question the committee sought to answer was whether Martha had "changed" during her imprisonment. One member went with the pastor to visit Martha in prison, and the entire committee met with a probation counselor who specialized in sex offenders. Members learned about the typical motivations of offenders. They also explored what precautions and restrictions should be in place with Martha's agreement if she returned to the church. The probation officer stated very directly that it was the church's responsibility to take Martha back.

Continuing discussions within the committee and the congregation made it clear that there were many unresolved feelings. In one meeting, the pastor challenged the congregation, saying that some of them had been "sweeping the situation under the rug." After twelve years, the rug had become very lumpy and people fell over it on their way into church. The pastor called for the church to begin a process of emotional healing.

As one step toward healing, Bev Eikenberry from the Ministry of Reconciliation, facilitated a congregational meeting focused on feelings. Church members were finally able to express strong feelings they had suppressed for twelve years. At that meeting, someone asked for a vote on whether to invite Martha to return to the church. Only a few people had participated in the discussion when this vote was requested. The pastor urged further discussion, cautioning that a premature vote, taken before everyone had an opportunity to speak, likely would split the church. He recommended that *everyone* express their opinion about the situation confronting the church and Martha.

One person commented: "Maybe another congregation could handle her better."

Then a person on the other side of the room said, "But maybe they wouldn't want her."

A third person said, "That wouldn't be very Christian of them."

The pastor allowed some silence after that expression, and then asked if everyone had heard the comments. Then he asked each of the three people to restate what they had said. The result was that many people started to shift their focus to *how* the congregation should welcome Martha back.

The committee developed a plan for Martha's return and wrote guidelines for her behavior and the church's response. One of the guidelines, which were based on state law, was that Martha would not attend church without an advocate along to accompany her through the building. Martha and her husband met with the deacons and signed an agreement to follow all the guidelines.

The committee publicized a special Wednesday evening service when Martha would worship with her congregation for the first time. Fifty people attended the service, which included time for discussion. Martha expressed her reactions and her needs, and so did many members. After a second Wednesday evening service, the congregation held a meeting to continue discussing Martha's re-entry. At this meeting, the pastor noted that some people would require additional time for healing but that other matters required the church's energy. It was time, he said, for Martha to start attending Sunday services and for the congregation to stop debating her return. When Martha began attending on Sundays, she limited her interactions with others to simple greetings. More recently, she has attended some adult Sunday school classes and a church potluck.

The pastor described one incident involving a longtime member of the church who could not accept Martha's return. This woman visited another church one Sunday but was very unhappy and unsatisfied with the experience. She returned to the congregation and told the pastor that she didn't like the other church and that she missed her own church. The pastor gently pointed out that her experience probably helped her understand better how Martha must feel.[10]

We have no fixed formula that will lead to a consensus about such painful and divisive issues. A process that works in one situation may fail in another. We would, however, define a good decision-making process as one that (a) honors God through prayerful attention to scripture and to the guidance of the Holy Spirit and (b) honors the perspectives and feelings of all the people involved.

Each member of a community brings a limited but valuable perspective, which is shaped by that person's life experiences. Since our perspectives are different, it is not surprising that we often hear God differently. A disagreement does not usually mean that one person is completely wrong and the other completely right. Often each side hears part of what God wants to say, a part that others may have ignored. Therefore, each side needs the other in order to hear God more completely. Since God often speaks through minority voices, strong dissent usually means that the process of discernment needs to continue. As people with different perspectives learn to communicate honestly and respectfully with one another, they become more likely to agree on a solution that honors the fullness of God's will.

The issue of abortion can illustrate the need for a respectful conversation between Christians with diverse perspectives. Some of us hear God saying we should protect the life of unborn children. Others hear God saying we should extend grace to women with unwanted pregnancies and protect the quality of life for those who are already born. The statement on abortion passed in 1984 by the Church of the Brethren Annual Conference attempts with some success to hear both sides of the debate and respond with integrity. It is brief enough to be quoted in full:

> Human life is a gracious gift from God who loves us.
>
> The Church of the Brethren opposes abortion because the rejection of unborn children violates the love by which God creates and nurtures human life.
>
> We recognize that our society contributes to unwanted pregnancies in many ways and gives too little care to those who must bear the consequences.
>
> We recognize also our responsibility to work for a caring society that undergirds women who choose to carry pregnancies

to full term, a caring society that treasures and nurtures all children, even the unborn, the unwanted, the unloved, a caring society that protects integrity of conscience in decision-making in relation to pregnancy and child bearing while also acting to protect the unborn.

We hold ourselves accountable to develop constructive, creative alternatives to abortion in the communities of which we are a part.

We grieve with all who struggle with difficult circumstances which lead some to consider abortion.

We encourage women and men caught in such struggles to seek the counsel and support of family members, trusted friends, spiritual leaders, and appropriate professionals in the Body of Christ, and to consider prayerfully the church's opposition to abortion.

We hold in love and will support those who choose to give birth to children, and the children themselves, as well as those who believe conscientiously they must terminate pregnancy.

We acknowledge our lack of compassion, our judgmentalism, and other sinful attitudes that separate us from the love by which God calls and redeems us.

We affirm our commitment, as in the 1972 statement on abortion and our historic peace position, to counsel with and to uphold one another, to maintain fellowship with those who differ, and to extend to others the compassion we receive from Christ.[11]

Donald Miller served on the study committee that took two years to complete this statement. He recalls that committee members held strong views on abortion, ranging from extremely liberal to extremely conservative. They agreed from the beginning that they would work by consensus, meaning that any member could veto a proposed wording. Members prayed and listened a great deal, and they grew in respect for one another in spite of their differences.[12] Eventually they agreed to a statement that a large majority of the delegates to Annual Conference could affirm. Nearly two decades later, this statement still has broad support within the denomination, although we must continue to ask how well we have followed through with the pledges it contains.

There are undoubtedly easier ways to make decisions than to search for agreement as described in this chapter. Dictatorial leaders can be

Story Starter: Building Consensus

Many churches handle routine business by consensus but shift to voting when an issue is challenging enough to generate differences of opinion. A church that seeks to practice Matthew 18:18-20 will strive for consensus even when dealing with difficult issues. Perhaps the church is considering a new approach for a stewardship emphasis for the year, a housing outreach project in the church's neighborhood, or a partnership with another organization or church to provide a service to the community. Whether the specific issue is something that has been addressed in the past or something new to the group, the consensus-building process should honor God through prayerful attention to scripture and to the guidance of the Holy Spirit. The process should also honor the perspectives and feelings of all the people involved.

When a church faces a difficult decision, the easiest way to build consensus may be to start with a representative committee or board. At the very beginning of the process, the committee should agree on a definition of "consensus." The committee may decide, for example, that unanimous agreement is required or that some disagreement is possible if those who disagree choose not to block committee action. Requiring consensus by either of these definitions takes time, but it also encourages trust because members know that a recommendation cannot be adopted without their consent. After the committee has gathered any needed information, the hard work of sharing perspectives and possible solutions can begin in earnest. It is important for members to think creatively so that possible solutions are not overlooked. The goal is not to find a "perfect" solution, but a specific proposal or action plan that everyone can support. If even one member objects, then the committee must continue discussing and revising their plan. When the committee reaches a consensus as they have defined it, then they can decide how to share their proposal with others.

Whether or not the consensus-building process feels successful, the committee should take time to evaluate it together. Each participant should be encouraged to answer the following questions aloud: Did everyone participate fully in the process? Was there a clear understanding of consensus? Was adequate time allowed for thorough study and discussion of the issues? Did the group pray about their work? Were all participants respected by the others on the committee? How did the process "feel"? How could it have been improved?

very efficient because they make decisions unilaterally. Individualism may reduce the need for shared authority because there is less to decide as a community; however, community life suffers when individuals all "do their own thing." Matthew does not accept either of these extremes but calls, instead, for prayerful discernment by the disciples as a community based on Jesus' promise to be present. If Jesus is patient enough to attend all our church meetings, we can be patient enough to listen for the messages he offers us through one another.

Questions for Discussion

1. How do you understand the promises Jesus makes in verses 18-20? Try to paraphrase each of them in your own words. Describe a situation from your own experience that exemplifies one of these promises.

2. How do you respond to the promise that "If two of you agree on earth about anything you ask, it will be done for you by my Father in heaven" (18:19)? Do you take this promise literally? Do you take it seriously?

3. How do you understand the relationship between humility and authority? Are these qualities inconsistent with one another, or can they be reconciled?

4. How have you experienced authority within the church? Have you experienced leaders who were too authoritarian, who lacked authority, or who succeeded in combining authority with humility? Have you experienced a congregation in which authority was shared along the lines suggested in this chapter? If so, please describe how this worked in your experience. If you have participated in more than one faith tradition, compare the ways in which authority is exercised in each tradition.

5. How do you define a consensus? What do you see as the advantages or disadvantages of seeking a consensus instead of just a majority vote?

6. What process would you use to build consensus on a difficult issue in your church? Which aspects of that process would be critical in any effort to build consensus? Which are specific to your situation?

NOTES

1. Andrew T. Lincoln, "Matthew—A Story for Teachers?" *The Bible in Three Dimensions,* eds. D. J. A. Clines, S. E. Fowl, and S. E. Porter (Sheffield: Sheffield Academic Press, 1990), 110; Mark Allen Powell, *God with Us: A Pastoral Theology of Matthew's Gospel* (Minneapolis: Augsburg Fortress, 1995), 87; Warren Carter and John Paul Heil, *Matthew's Parables: Audience Oriented Perspectives* (CBQMS, 30; Washington: Catholic Biblical Association, 1998), 114.

2. Powell, *God with Us,* 68.

3. Raymond E. Brown, Karl P. Donfried, and John Reumann, *Peter in the New Testament* (Minneapolis, Minn.; Augsburg Publishing House, 1973), 78; Jack Dean Kingsbury, "The Figure of Peter in Matthew's Gospel as a Theological Problem," *Journal of Biblical Literature* 98 (1979), 71-73.

4. See Julius R. Mantey, "Distorted Translations in John 20:23; Matthew 16:18-19 and 18:18," *Review and Expositor: A Baptist Theological Journal* 78 (1981), 411; J. Duncan M. Derrett, "Binding and Loosing (Matt. 16:19; 18:18; John 29:23), *Journal of Biblical Literature* 102 (1983), 112-13.

5. Theodore W. Jennings, Jr., *Life as Worship: Prayer and Praise in Jesus' Name* (Grand Rapids: Eerdmans, 1982), 39.

6. Craig S. Keener, *A Commentary on the Gospel of Matthew* (Grand Rapids: Eerdmans, 1999), 455.

7. Allen T. Hansell, letter to the authors, June 22, 2000.

8. Don Fitzkee, "Harrisburg First: Hummel Street Is Its Home," *Messenger* (July 1993), 22-25.

9. Irvin Heishman, interview with Dan Ulrich, December 3, 2001 (quotation edited for length).

10. This account is based on telephone conversations in November 2001 between Jan Fairchild and Allen Kahler, the pastor of the congregation. The church board later approved the publication of the story. The board decided to include the church's name but to withhold "Martha's" as a witness to the reconciliation that has occurred.

11. Statement on Abortion adopted by 1984 Church of the Brethren Annual Conference. Accessed on the Internet at http://www.brethren.org/ac/ac_statements/abortion.htm, December 18, 2001.

12. Donald Miller, interview with Dan Ulrich, December 18, 2001.

9

Unlimited Forgiveness
Matthew 18:21-35

21 Then Peter came and said to him, "Lord, if another member of the church sins against me, how often should I forgive? As many as seven times?" 22 Jesus said to him, "Not seven times, but, I tell you, seventy-seven times.

23 "For this reason the kingdom of heaven may be compared to a king who wished to settle accounts with his slaves. 24 When he began the reckoning, one who owed him ten thousand talents was brought to him; 25 and, as he could not pay, his lord ordered him to be sold, together with his wife and children and all his possessions, and payment to be made. 26 So the slave fell on his knees before him, saying, 'Have patience with me, and I will pay you everything.' 27 And out of pity for him, the lord of that slave released him and forgave him the debt. 28 But that same slave, as he went out, came upon one of his fellow slaves who owed him a hundred denarii; and seizing him by the throat, he said, 'Pay what you owe.' 29 Then his fellow slave fell down and pleaded with him, 'Have patience with me, and I will pay you.' 30 But he refused; then he went and threw him into prison until he would pay the debt. 31 When his fellow slaves saw what had happened, they were greatly distressed, and they went and reported to their lord all that had taken place. 32 Then his lord summoned him and said to him, 'You wicked slave! I forgave you all that debt because you pleaded with me. 33 Should you not have had mercy on your fellow slave, as I had mercy on you?' 34 And in anger his lord handed him over to be tortured until he would pay his entire debt. 35 So my heavenly Father will also do to every one of you, if you do not forgive your brother or sister from your heart."

The Biblical Story

We move now to the final elaboration in Matthew 18 on the theme that humble people are great in God's reign. In 18:21-35, the focus shifts to forgiveness as an aspect of humility. Peter's question about forgiveness does not introduce an entirely new theme, because it is related to the instructions and promises in 18:15-20. After hearing those instructions, Peter wants Jesus to clarify what should happen if a member of the church (literally, a "brother") sins against him repeatedly. At what point should repeat offenses lead Peter to "bind" instead of "loose" someone's sins?

Peter's presence in 18:21 might come as a surprise for first-time readers. Jesus tells him to go fishing in 17:27 and, according to 18:1, the disciples ask their question at the same hour. The chronology makes better sense in Greek, however, because 17:27 could be translated, "*When* you go to the sea, cast a hook." Jesus does not tell Peter to go immediately, and in light of 18:21, we can assume that he is still around.

Although Peter's question sounds reasonable at one level, it is disappointing for anyone who has been paying attention to the story. We have observed that Matthew 18 is an urgent attempt by Jesus to resolve his conflict with the disciples by convincing them to adopt his view of greatness, including his posture as a servant. When Jesus warns the disciples that they need to repent (18:3), he is obeying his own teaching about direct communication. Jesus has experienced Peter as a stumbling block, so the warnings in 18:6-9 are especially relevant for Peter. Equally relevant are Jesus' words of grace, including his promise to remain with the disciples in spite of everything that could (and will) go wrong.

Given the urgency of Jesus' message, there is suspense about how the disciples will respond. Will they hear Jesus' message and repent, or will their ears and minds stay closed? The beginning of verse 21 is encouraging. The verb translated "came" has a deeper meaning for Matthew, who uses it whenever people approach Jesus with faith and reverence. In addition, Peter uses the title "Lord," which normally leads into a humble request or confession. After such a beginning, readers could hope for a continuation like, "Lord, have mercy because I have been an obstacle to you! Save me from the fate that is worse than drowning in the depths of the sea!" (cf. 14:30). Another good possibility would be, "Lord, have mercy because I am not worthy to have you come under my roof!" (cf. 8:8).[1]

As a response to Jesus' confrontive words, Peter's question feels out of place at best and arrogant at worst. Indeed, Matthew's irony is intense at this point. Peter presumes he will be the innocent victim of repeated sins by others. He does not realize that he himself will sin dreadfully and repeatedly against Jesus. If Peter understood the truth about himself, he would not seek a limit on forgiveness. His presumption stands out even more if we read verse 15 without the words "against you" (see NRSV margin). In that case Peter is the one who introduces the idea that the sin will be "against me" (18:21). Either way, Peter's question reveals that he has not really heard Jesus.

The word for "forgive" in 18:21-35 (*aphiēmi*) can be translated "let go," "release," or "cancel" (in the sense of canceling a debt). For Matthew, then, forgiving sins means releasing them so they no longer stand in the way of a right relationship. Forgiveness also involves letting go of the right to punish someone or seek revenge. The key words "forgive" and "brother" help to unify 18:21-35 by appearing at the beginning and end of the passage.[2]

Peter's proposal of a seven-strike limit on forgiveness sounds generous in light of Amos 1:1–2:11 and Job 33:29, which suggest that God will forgive the same nation or person three times but not four.[3] Even so, the proposal does not satisfy Jesus, who calls for forgiveness up to "seventy-seven times" or "seventy times seven" depending on the translation. Either way, the point is that the disciples should not count offenses. The large number alludes to Genesis 4:24, where Lamech boasts that he will get vengeance without limit. Jesus commands the disciples to counteract the cycle of vengeance by practicing unlimited forgiveness.[4]

Whereas 18:22 answers Peter's question directly, 18:23-35 does so indirectly in the form of a parable. Although the parable is not specifically about *repeated* sins, it is still relevant. It provides a compelling motive for forgiveness, and it confronts the attitude that leads Peter to ask for a limit.

Essentially, the parable dramatizes a saying that follows the Lord's Prayer: "If you forgive others their trespasses, your heavenly Father will also forgive you; but if you do not forgive others, neither will your Father forgive your trespasses" (6:14-15). The drama has three scenes, each with two main characters. Each scene consists of an introduction, a speech, and a resulting action:[5]

	Scene One	Scene Two	Scene Three
Introduction	18:23-25	18:28	18:31
Speech	18:26	18:29	18:32-33
Action	18:27	18:30	18:34

The similarities between these scenes makes their differences stand out even more. For example, Scenes One and Two feature almost identical pleas for mercy. This similarity highlights the stark differences between the amounts owed and the responses of the creditors. The slave in Scene One owes 10,000 talents, which is a huge debt because it combines the largest unit of money (talent) with the largest number in the Greek language (10,000). The modern equivalent would be "billions and billions of dollars." Since the story is exaggerated for effect, there is no need to ask whether a first-century slave could really owe so much. (The most realistic possibility would be a slave in charge of collecting taxes for an emperor.) The second debtor, who appears in Scene Two, owes 100 denarii or 100 days' wages for a laborer. That debt is the ancient equivalent of a used-car loan—substantial but not impossible to repay. When the 10,000 talent debtor ludicrously begs for more time, the master exceeds his wildest hopes by forgiving the entire debt. The slave is no longer under pressure to repay. Therefore, it is especially shocking when he refuses to heed the same plea for mercy from a fellow slave who owes much less.[6]

Scene Three combines aspects of the two previous scenes. The participants are the same as in Scene One, but the outcome is similar to that of Scene Two. An important variation in Scene Three is that the slave has no opportunity to plead for mercy. Instead, the master immediately pronounces judgment, bringing the parable to a conclusion. The unforgiving servant is condemned for his lack of mercy and treated just as he treated his fellow servant. The sentence of torture "until he would pay the debt" (18:34) echoes the length of the imprisonment in Scene Two (18:30). Although the slave's family is not punished in Scene Three, torture is a more severe punishment than being sold (18:25). This contrast with Scene One highlights the tragic consequence of the slave's failure to extend mercy to others.

The concluding verse brings this tragedy home to Peter, the other disciples, and Matthew's readers (18:35). The king and master in the parable represents God, whose mercy is so enormous that one can never earn or repay it. Still, God's mercy comes with the obligation to extend mercy to others. The failure to meet that obligation will result in a withdrawal of God's mercy.

If the master in the parable represents God, then the slaves represent disciples. Most of the parable invites its listeners to identify with the fellow slaves mentioned in 18:31. Those slaves are "greatly distressed" at the behavior of the 10,000 talent debtor, which is exactly how any reasonable listener would feel.[7] Even so, the conclusion of the parable in 18:35 presses the listener into a far less comfortable role. Jesus asks them to identify with the 10,000 talent debtor, saying the debtor's plight will become theirs if they fail to forgive one another from the heart.

The word "you" in 18:35 is plural, so the parable is not aimed at Peter alone; nevertheless, he is an appropriate target because his earlier question is so presumptuous. If Peter learns to think of himself as the 10,000 talent debtor, then he will be humbler and more ready for his role at the end of Matthew's story. Peter will receive an astounding gift of forgiveness at Jesus' resurrection, and he will need to know that the gift comes with an important string attached.

As Jesus confronts Peter, he is opposing one kind of forgiveness and supporting another. Jesus does not want Peter (or anyone else) to hand down pardons with an air of superiority. That sort of forgiveness is not a gracious gift, but an attempt to gain honor at another's expense. Instead, Jesus expects forgiveness to be the fruit of humility. Real forgiveness happens when people extend to others the grace they have already received from God. God's grace is the soil in which humility and forgiveness grow best.

Unfortunately, the disciples seem to miss Jesus' point, and Matthew hints at their lack of understanding a few verses later. In 19:8 Jesus declares to the Pharisees that Moses allowed men to divorce their wives "because you were so hardhearted." The phrase translated "hardhearted" echoes Jesus' command to "forgive . . . from your heart," and it suggests that divorce is due to a lack of forgiveness. When the disciples overhear Jesus' teaching, they object that it would be better to remain single than to marry with no possibility of divorce (19:10). Jesus approves of singleness, but the disciples' objection suggests that they share the Pharisees' hardheartedness. They cannot see marriage as a good gift from God unless there is a way out. Jesus responds that not everyone can accept the disciples' teaching that it is better not to marry (19:11). Some people need to marry, and they especially need to practice the art of unlimited forgiveness.

We have considered some of what Matthew 18:21-35 says in context. Now we must deal with something it does not say. There is no explicit requirement that an offender must repent in order to be forgiven, and this omission has led to a debate among scholars.[8] Those who argue for an assumed requirement of repentance point out that an offender must "listen" in order to be won back as a brother or sister (18:15-17). Since Peter is asking for a clarification of 18:15-20, his question and Jesus' response assume the conditions outlined before. In addition, both debtors in the parable show signs of repentance in that they plead for mercy and promise to repay. At the end of the parable, the master emphasizes that he forgave the first debtor in response to his plea for mercy (18:32). Moreover, there are other points in the story where Jesus insists that those who have sinned must repent or face God's judgment (e.g., 18:3, 6-9).

If Matthew 18:21-35 presupposes repentance, then the command to "let such a one be to you as a Gentile and a tax collector" (18:17) and the command to forgive without limit (18:22) address different situations. The offender in 18:17 has rejected repeated calls for repentance by other disciples. The community is eager to forgive but will not do so until the offender repents. In contrast, the offender in 18:21-22 has repeatedly sinned, repented, and sinned again. In that case, Jesus commands the community to forgive every time the offender repents.

On the other hand, scholars who argue for unconditional forgiveness point out that Matthew 18:21-35 is one of several passages about forgiveness that do not mention repentance (6:14-15; 9:2). Perhaps forgiveness is not just a desired result of the visits commanded in 18:15-17, but an essential preparation for anyone who would try to win back a brother or sister. Even the decision to treat someone as a Gentile and a tax collector would need to be made in a spirit of forgiveness. This interpretation avoids the thorny problem of deciding whether an offender has repented sincerely or not. Even if the offender's repentance is insincere, the community must forgive. A drawback of this interpretation is that it is not easy to reconcile the community's power to "bind" with a requirement that the community forgive unconditionally.

Although we lean toward the view that Matthew 18:21-35 presupposes repentance, we want to emphasize several points on which both sides can agree. First, disciples who try to correct others should be willing, indeed eager, to forgive. That attitude mirrors the compassion of the shepherd in 18:10-14, and it is an important step on the path toward full forgiveness. Second, forgiveness is clearly required whenever an offender repents. According to Matthew 18:23-35, withholding forgiveness at that point is a sin that jeopardizes one's own relationship with God. Third, Matthew 18 does not prohibit forgiveness, not even in situations where an offender is unrepentant or unavailable. Many victims of sin find inner peace only when they are able to release their bitter feelings against those who hurt them. Matthew 18 leaves the door open for that kind of release.

Regardless of whether Matthew 18:21-35 presupposes repentance, it is clear that 18:15-20 and 18:21-35 belong together. Without honest communication about what has happened, words of forgiveness are often superficial. Church discipline without a spirit of forgiveness can become oppressive; the same is true, however, when the church teaches unlimited forgiveness but fails to witness firmly against chronic sins like racism, economic injustice, and family violence. The victims of these and other sins need the support of caring, assertive communities of faith.[9]

In Matthew's time, there was no legal protection for children or slaves who were abused by the head of a household.[10] An abused wife might get some help from her family of origin, but even that was unlikely. The house churches of Matthew's time did not have the power to change the social structures that allowed abuse. They could, however, confront the abuser, either as a disciple in need of correction or as an unbeliever in need of conversion. Churches could also "bind" the abuse, stating to everyone involved that it was not God's will. We do not know how often that kind of support took place in the early church, but Matthew 18:15-20 clearly calls for it.

In Matthew 18, Jesus calls the disciples to balance their concern for disciples who have sinned with concern for the victims of sin. Part of that balance is a command to forgive every offender who repents and to do so as often as they repent. By forgiving without limits, the disciples can humbly extend to others the grace they have received.

Our Stories

"Often it's not the boulder in the path that keeps us from reaching our goal; it's the pebble in the shoe." That anonymous proverb speaks volumes about the need for unlimited forgiveness. Most of us have habits that are irritating to others. Without constant communication and forgiveness, the irritation can grow into resentment, and resentment can build to the point that it destroys a relationship. If forgiveness were limited to even 490 offenses, no one could live or work together for very long. Whenever we feel a "pebble in the shoe," we need to stop and talk it out.[11]

Practice with forgiving pebble-sized offenses can prepare us to handle an occasional boulder. Huge offenses happen from time to time, and how one responds to them can make the difference between unending bitterness or abiding joy. In three of the most heartwarming stories we received, people forgave horrible sins in heroic ways.

The first of these stories comes from Steve Clapp:

> One of the most meaningful instances of forgiveness I have observed was near my hometown in downstate Illinois during my college years. On homecoming night a young high school couple was in a tragic automobile accident. I'll call them Brad and Alice for the purposes of this account. They had been dating for three years, and most people assumed they would get married. Brad's father had died a few years earlier, and his mother worked long hours at a low paying job. Brad spent a lot of time at Alice's home, enjoying the closeness of her family.
>
> That tragic night, Brad had been drinking. Alice had not, but unfortunately Brad was the one driving. He tried to get across a railroad track before an oncoming train reached the intersection, and he lost the contest.
>
> The way that the train hit the car killed Alice instantly, but Brad was thrown from the car and survived, though he sustained injuries. A few days later he left the hospital without his physician's permission in order to attend Alice's funeral. Filled with self-contempt and sure her family would not want to

see him, he sat at the back of the church and later stood at the cemetery far back from the other mourners.

After the words at the graveside service were concluded, Alice's father noticed Brad and started walking toward him. Brad wanted to run but stood in place, feeling that her father had the right to do or say anything that he wanted. When he reached Brad, Alice's father put an arm around him and said, "I've lost my only child. You lost your father. It looks to me like we need each other." That act of forgiveness changed the whole course of Brad's life.[12]

A second story comes from Matt Guynn, who at the time was serving with Christian Peacemaker Teams in Chiapas, Mexico. *Las Abejas* means "The Bees" in Spanish. It is the name chosen by a close-knit community of Mayan Christians, who have supported one another in the midst of poverty and persecution. The *Abejas* take the gospel call to "love your enemies" very seriously and witness publicly that their Christian commitment means they will not kill, though they are ready to die. Matt accompanied the *Abejas* as they returned to a village where they had been terrorized by paramilitary forces a few years earlier. The *Abejas* left before anyone died, but some of their homes were burned to the ground:

> "He's one of the people who drove us from our home," said our host, a member of the pacifist group *Las Abejas*. On the Puebla basketball court, we had been approached by an energetic thirty-something man, who chatted for a while and then invited us to visit his home the next morning. Our *Abejas* host decided to join us for the meeting.
>
> The next morning we arrived at the home of the alleged paramilitary. He offered us refreshments and we talked about coffee prices, about his family, and finally about the 1997 conflict that tore this community of 250 families apart. "We went off the path," he said, "and we need to go back and find our way again, so that we can move ahead together toward the kingdom of God." The conversation turned to scripture and the instructions there about right living.
>
> "Which of scripture's commandments do you find hardest to follow?" I asked.

Without missing a beat, he answered, "Loving my neighbor." Then he shared, "Some of us are repenting now," and he turned to talk to our *Abejas* accompanier, "I haven't talked to you in months, or years." And again he said, "We went off the path here in Puebla."

I asked if we could pray together, CPTers with *Abeja* with paramilitary, and, standing, we made a circle in his house and prayed aloud. Afterward, we all sang and played praise songs together for forty-five minutes.

"I believed what he said about repentance," our *Abejas* host said after we were back at his home.

Doing patrols this week in this Mayan community where divisions and past hurts prevent some from looking each other in the eye, I thought, "Who are the people in my own community that I will not look in the eye?"

As the drums of war are pounding in the United States, who is it that you will not speak to? Where do religious and political divisions or discomfort with the Other (Arab, gay or lesbian, poor . . .) prevent you from unity in your own hometown? Take hope from this member of the *Abejas*, willing to pray and sing with his former persecutor.[13]

Matt wrote this story shortly after September 11, 2001, when terrorists used hijacked airliners as missiles, killing thousands of people in New York, northern Virginia, and Pennsylvania. About a month later, the United States entered the civil war in Afghanistan in an attempt to capture or kill the people who planned the attacks. As we write, the alleged mastermind, Osama bin Laden, has eluded capture, and most Americans are still furious enough to want justice by any means our government considers necessary. We are all afraid that terrorists will attack again, and we are frustrated because no one, including the U.S. military, has a plan that can guarantee our safety. While Americans are proud of the firefighters and others who gave their lives for others, we grieve along with the families of those who were so cruelly killed.

Of the many heroic stories that have emerged from that tragedy, Kim Statkevicus's example is especially relevant for this book.

Kim and her husband, Derek, had a loving marriage, a beautiful son, and another child on the way. On September 11, Derek was working at the World Trade Center. He did not survive. In the months since then, Kim has grieved for Derek and dealt with the myriad changes that accompany single parenthood. Through it all she has relied more than ever on her faith in God. In a recent telephone conversation, she said, "I never considered myself to have such a strong faith, but when Derek died, I kept praying 'The Serenity Prayer.' I knew that God would not give me more than I could handle, so I just gave it all up to him from the beginning."

Kim's faith is strong, partly because she has the support of a loving church and a non-denominational Bible study fellowship. As Kim was praying after the attacks, she remembered the discussion in her Bible study group about Matthew 5:44: "But I say to you, Love your enemies and pray for those who persecute you." So she began to pray for the terrorists who had killed her husband and for all other terrorists. Whenever she remembers them, she continues to pray that they will open their hearts to God and find peace. She also asks God to work through her and to use her as a witness. She hopes her prayers and testimony can make some difference in the world, so that others will not have to suffer. She said, "Who knows who I will touch. Maybe even one of the attackers."

There can be no doubt that God has answered Kim's prayer to be a witness. Friends were amazed at her commitment to pray for the terrorists. Word got around, and she has had many opportunities to share about her experience and her faith. God has answered her prayers in other ways, too. Many of the kindnesses she has shared with others are now being returned, and God continues to give her strength day by day. "God's blessings are amazing," she said. "My new life is hard, but God has returned good to me a thousandfold." When Kim was asked whether she had forgiven the attackers, she hesitated for a moment and then said, "Yeah. I've forgiven them. I feel sorry for them because Satan got hold of them. I needed to forgive them because I don't want my children to grow up with hatred for anyone."[14]

Kim's example of forgiveness goes beyond the requirements of Matthew 18:21-35. As we have seen, that passage is about forgiving a brother or sister, which for Matthew means a fellow disciple. The passage also probably assumes that the disciple is repentant, and we have no indication of repentance on the part of the attackers. Nevertheless, Matthew's larger story calls for forgiveness to be extended beyond the community of disciples. In 28:16-20, Jesus challenges the disciples to make disciples of all nations. The essence of that task will be to share Jesus' offer of forgiveness and transformation with anyone and everyone. Faithful witnesses like Kim still share Jesus' message of forgiveness in the hope that God can change even the worst of sinners—even Peter, Saul, and Osama.

Our point is not that Osama bin Laden and his followers will no longer threaten us if we choose to forgive them. Some people must be restrained, if possible, so they cannot go on hurting others; but restraining and killing are two different things. Killing is inconsistent with evangelism, partly because it cuts short the opportunity to repent. After Christians have gone to war, evangelism becomes much more difficult among the nations who were once their enemies. Memories of past crusades make it especially hard for Muslims to accept the gospel, and a new crusade is not likely to help.

Although the Bush administration no longer refers to its war on terrorism as a "crusade," we still see in the United States the arrogance that leads to crusades. If North American Christians believe that we are qualified to carry out God's judgment against evildoers, then we have something in common with the small minority of Muslims who kill in the name of Allah. This situation makes interfaith forgiveness especially urgent as well as difficult. Short of Christ's return, the best hope for lasting peace in much of the world depends on mutual forgiveness among Muslims, Christians, and Jews.

Whether forgiveness takes place at an international level or an interpersonal one, it is often a prayerful journey rather than a momentary decision. After suffering a serious wrong, we may feel we lack the strength to even begin such a journey, but God answers prayers for that kind of strength. As we pray, we can share any feeling we like with God, perhaps using the psalms of lament as a way to express our grief and anger. We can continue to speak the truth as we have experienced it, telling God and others about our sense of pain, bitterness, and betrayal. Eventually we may come to the point where we can sincerely ask God to bless and forgive those who have hurt us. At that point God may show us an opportunity to offer them our forgiveness face to face.

We may find that one "I forgive" is not enough. We may need to repeat that prayer many times before we begin to feel the anger and bitterness slip away. If our prayers lead to a humble attitude before God, we may realize that our own actions have not been perfect and that we need to ask forgiveness as well as give it.

If we need time to journey toward forgiveness, the same may be true for the people we have wronged. It may take time for anger to dissipate or for others to trust that our repentance is real. Others may sin against us by failing to practice Jesus' call for unlimited forgiveness. We cannot force them to forgive, but we can forgive their hardheartedness, if necessary. Most of all, we can trust God to forgive all who repent, even when human beings are slow to follow suit.

This story, contributed by Ed Poling, shows that real forgiveness can be worth the wait:

> Upon moving to a new congregation, I got to know a special family. Three sisters, along with their husbands and children, were active members of the church. Over the course of time, I learned of a painful past—their parents had divorced while the girls were growing up. Their feelings of disappointment, anger, and resentment toward their dad festered over the years. But the sisters stuck together and gained strength from their church family, trusting that God would help them to forgive. Now their mom was elderly, but still a part of the church. Their dad had not been in church for years, though he still lived close by.
>
> While serving as their pastor, I witnessed the blossoming of grace. Just as Jesus counseled Peter not to pass judgment on others, so this family gradually let go of its hurts. The elderly father began attending church once again with his daughters. What a treat it was to see them all sit together. Eventually he rejoined and was warmly welcomed by the congregation. Perhaps it was the parents' advancing age and declining health. Perhaps it was the daughters' need to become their parents. Or perhaps it was the congregation's welcoming spirit. In any case somewhere along the way a new sense of unity emerged.
>
> At the father's funeral last year, the oldest daughter chronicled his life with words of appreciation, recalling "a man who enabled me to bring peace to our relationship." What a change! It was an act of forgiveness seventy-seven times over.[15]

We cannot leave the topic of unlimited forgiveness without returning to the problem discussed in chapter one. We argued there that earlier generations in the Church of the Brethren took Matthew 18:15-17 out of context and sometimes used it to support a kind of discipline that was often neither loving nor redemptive. That history may seem far behind us, but old wounds remain and may still require forgiveness. In the following story, Jim Benedict shares a gift of forgiveness even though the people most directly involved had passed away:

There was a knock at my door. I thought perhaps the women's group needed help setting up tables and chairs, or maybe there was a question about the order of service, or—more likely— someone just wanted to stick their head in and say hi. "Come in," I said. And thus began one of the most interesting . . . encounters I have had in nearly fifteen years of full-time ministry.

It was an older gentleman I didn't recognize. He was wearing a wrinkled suit and an old-fashioned, narrow tie. He had a thick shock of white hair, a big smile, and a suitcase in each hand. He also had a story to tell. It was a long story, which came out in bits and pieces, some of them repeated a couple of times.

One hundred and fifty years ago this man's great-grandfather was an elder in a neighboring Brethren congregation. The elder's daughter, my visitor's grandmother, was raised in the church and eventually married a young man who was also Brethren. For a time, the younger couple was faithful and active in the life of the church. But then the elder's son-in-law got the notion to go to a county fair—an activity frowned upon as "worldly" by the congregation.

When word got out that the young man had attended the fair, he and his wife were visited by deacons and the man was admonished. Angered by the confrontation and headstrong (according to his grandson), the young man decided to leave the church rather than seek reconciliation. Torn between faithfulness to her church and to her spouse, the elder's daughter soon followed her husband out of the church.

Years later, when my visitor was just a young boy, his father (son of the fair-going man) died in the flu epidemic and the boy was sent to live with these grandparents who by this time had been separated from the Brethren for more than a quarter century. But the boy's grandmother still held the Brethren faith in

Story Starter: Keeping a Spiritual Journal

A spiritual journal is a valuable tool as one journeys toward forgiveness. In *How to Keep a Spiritual Journal: A Guide to Journal-Keeping for Inner Growth and Personal Discovery*, Ronald Klug writes: "A journal is a tool for self-discovery, aid to concentration, mirror of the soul, a place to generate and capture ideas, a safety valve for the emotions, a training ground for the writer, and a good friend and confidant."[17] If you do not already write a spiritual journal, why not try one? Write your thoughts, prayers, and feelings in a private notebook. Be as brief as necessary, but discipline yourself to pray regularly and to write something each day.

As you practice daily prayer and journaling, identify a person you need to forgive. Write your thoughts and feelings about the situation. Then include that person in your prayers every day for at least two weeks. Pray that God will bless that person in whatever way God chooses. After two weeks of prayer, write in your journal what you learned from this prayer experience. Describe your feelings for the person. Have your feelings changed? In what ways? Do you *feel* more forgiving? Did you gain a new understanding about the person or the circumstances?

Based on what you have learned through two weeks of general prayers, you may decide to focus your prayers in more specific ways. For example, you might pray for your acceptance of the person or your readiness to forgive. You might choose to continue to pray for blessings in the person's life. Pray each day for two more weeks, and write in your journal about your second prayer experience. Are you ready to forgive the person? If not, can you continue to pray about forgiveness? Do you have concerns you feel unable to address alone? Are these concerns for which you can seek guidance from another (perhaps your pastor, a spiritual director, or a counselor)? If you are ready to forgive, can you go to the person and express your forgiveness directly? Write in your journal about your experience of extending forgiveness.

high regard. In many ways it remained her faith; none other could replace it. She taught her grandson about Brethren beliefs and practiced as much of the faith as she could apart from a congregation. She also passed along her regret about the break with the congregation and the pain it still caused her.

My visitor explained that this time with his grandmother had been mostly forgotten as he had gone on to college, spent forty years as a pilot for a major airline, and raised two daughters of his own. But in the last few years, he found himself thinking about it often. It felt like a wound that was crying out for healing. Finally, at age eighty-seven, he decided to try to do something about it. Because he was legally blind, he asked his wife to drive him to the bus station. There he purchased the tickets and transfers for an eight-hundred-mile journey. With layovers the trip had taken twenty-three hours. Then there was a forty-five minute taxi ride from a nearby city to my small town church.

After hearing the man's story, I was able to find an older deacon couple who had an idea where this man's grandmother had lived as a girl. We took a drive to that farm and described what he could not see. Then we went to the old meetinghouse where his great-grandfather had been an elder. My visitor was grateful, almost overwhelmed.

There was only one more thing he wanted. Hesitantly, he said, "My grandmother was such a wonderful lady, a Christian lady. Is there a way . . . could you . . . forgive her?" I had no precedent, but I did not hesitate. We bowed in prayer, and in the name of the Church of the Brethren I reclaimed a long lost sister.[16]

Questions for Discussion

1. Does "forgiveness as an aspect of humility" increase your understanding of either forgiveness or humility? What aspects of humility are enhanced by forgiveness? How is forgiveness enriched by humility?
2. Does the parable "feel" different to you when you experience it from the perspective of different characters? Is one feeling more "contemporary" or "real" for your life than others? How do you explain this difference?

3. Is repentance a necessary condition for forgiveness? How can people evaluate the sincerity of repentance? What are the pitfalls of judging the sincerity of repentance?

4. Do you agree that direct communication and forgiveness belong together? If not, discuss how you can forgive without direct communication. If you agree, elaborate on how you understand the relationship between forgiveness and direct communication.

5. Think of a personal experience in which you struggled to balance your concern for a person who had sinned and your concern for someone else who was hurt by the sin. Were you able to forgive? Was the victim able to forgive? How did you balance these two conflicting concerns?

6. If someone you loved was the victim of a terrorist bombing, would you feel called by Christ to forgive the perpetrators? How do you respond to the authors' comments regarding Osama bin Laden?

7. The authors suggest that forgiveness is often a journey rather than a momentary decision. Have you experienced forgiveness as a journey? How is time a factor in that type of forgiveness? Have there been times when you forgave someone quickly? What factors made that possible for you? If you can remember instances of each type of forgiveness, compare them.

8. Have you sought forgiveness from God or from someone else? If so, did you feel forgiven? How have your experiences of forgiveness affected your ability to forgive others?

NOTES

1. Note, based on 17:25, that Peter's house in Capernaum is probably the setting for Matthew 18. After mentioning Peter's house (8:14-15), Matthew often refers to "the house" in Capernaum without indicating the owner (9:10, 28; 13:1, 36; 17:25). The lack of further information suggests that it is the same house mentioned previously. Another detail consistent with this view is that Peter's mother-in-law repeatedly or continually serves Jesus after her healing (8:15).

2. William G. Thompson, *Matthew's Advice to a Divided Community, Mt. 17, 22–18, 35* (Rome: Biblical Institute Press, 1970), 162, 223.

3. Donald Senior, "Matthew 18:21-35," *Interpretation* 41 (1987), 403-7.

4. W. D. Davies and Dale C. Allison, Jr., *A Critical and Exegetical Commentary on the Gospel According to Saint Matthew*, vol. 2 (Edinburgh: T & T Clark, 1991), 793.

5. Thompson, *Advice*, 211.

6. Thompson, *Advice,* 217; Bernard Brandon Scott, "The King's Accounting: Matthew 18:23-34," *Journal of Biblical Literature* 104 (1985), 438.

7. Matthew uses the same word to describe the disciples' distress at hearing that Jesus will be killed (17:23).

8. Frederick Dale Bruner, *Matthew: A Commentary* (Dallas: Word Publishing, 1990), vol. 2, 656, argues that Matthew 18:21-35 presupposes repentance on the part of the offender. Davies and Allison, *Matthew*, vol. 2, 792, argue the opposite.

9. Elaine Ramshaw, "Power and Forgiveness in Matthew 18," *Word and World* 18 (1998), 403.

10. Thomas Wiedemann, *Adults and Children in the Roman Empire* (New Haven: Yale University Press, 1989), 28.

11. For helpful, though different, pastoral perspectives on forgiveness, see Johann Christoph Arnold, *Seventy Times Seven: The Power of Forgiveness* (Farmington, Pa.: The Plough Publishing House, 1997); and David Augsburger, *Caring Enough to Forgive: True Forgiveness* and *Caring Enough to Not Forgive: False Forgiveness* (Scottdale, Pa.: Herald Press, 1981).

12. Steve Clapp, e-mail communication to Jan Fairchild, December 2, 2000.

13. Matt Guynn, "Chiapas: Praying with the Paramilitary Other," e-mailed to Dan Ulrich, September 16, 2001.

14. Kim Statkevicus, telephone interview with Dan Ulrich, January 25, 2002. "The Serenity Prayer" ("God, give [me] grace to accept with serenity . . .") was composed by Reinhold Niebuhr in 1943.

15. Edward Poling, e-mail communication to Jan Fairchild, November 6, 2001.

16. Jim Benedict, quoted in *The Love Feast*, comp. Frank Ramirez (Elgin, Ill.: Brethren Press, 2000), 28-29.

17. Ronald Klug, *How to Keep a Spiritual Journal: A Guide to Journal-Keeping for Inner Growth and Personal Discovery* (Minneapolis: Augsburg Fortress, 1993), 11.

Life with Jesus
Matthew 18:20; Matthew 28:20

For where two or three are gathered in my name, I am there among them (Matt. 18:20).

And remember, I am with you always, to the end of the age (Matt. 28:20).

We have already noted that Jesus' ongoing presence with the disciples is a major theme in Matthew's story. The story begins with the name "Emmanuel," meaning "God is with us" (1:23) and ends with a climactic promise by the risen Jesus to be with the disciples in their mission (28:20). Because of this strategic repetition, Jesus' promise to be with those who gather in his name stands out like a tower of hope among the more challenging aspects of Matthew 18.

Taking Stock

The main task of this chapter is to explore the hope Jesus offers through his gift of presence, but first it is time to draw some preliminary conclusions. This book interprets Matthew 18 in light of its historical background and literary context. Regarding the historical background, we concluded that traveling missionaries probably recited Matthew's story from beginning to end in the households that welcomed them. If the hosts accepted the missionaries' challenge to repent and follow Jesus, then the same story became a vehicle for training in discipleship. This background helps account for many aspects of the story, including Matthew's emphasis on mission. It also suggests that Matthew's earliest readers often heard speeches like Matthew 18 in the context of a larger story.

Taken out of context, Matthew 18 may sound like a set of rules for life within the church. In context, however, it sounds like an urgent attempt by Jesus to resolve a sharp, ongoing conflict with the disciples. Jesus needs to correct the disciples' misunderstanding and arrogance so they will continue his mission in his way: as humble servants. Nevertheless, the disciples do not understand Jesus' teaching on humility, so their conflict with him escalates. By the end of the story, they are like the debtor who owes 10,000 talents. Forgiven by Jesus, they must forgive others. It is evident, then, that Matthew 18 and the larger story help to interpret one another. Matthew 18 is not an isolated set of instructions, but an integral part of the story as a whole.

The theme and structure of Matthew 18 became clearer through a comparison with the Sermon on the Mount. Both speeches state their themes in similar terms and then elaborate. The overall theme of Matthew 18 is that humble people are greatest in the reign of heaven. Matthew 18:1-4 presents the theme, and 18:5-35 is a series of elaborations. In our study of the elaborations, we highlighted Matthew's teaching regarding hospitality, self-discipline, compassionate searching, direct communication, shared authority, and forgiveness. We observed that these values are each related to humility as understood by Matthew.

Jesus models these values in Matthew's story. Although Jesus is the rightful heir to the throne of David, he willingly accepts a humble status, first as a fleeing child and then as a suffering servant. As an adult, Jesus welcomes needy people, including children, with extraordinary grace. Although he is genuinely tempted to take an easier course, he obeys God's will to the point of dying on a cross, constantly saying no to Satan, even when tempted by means of a close follower. Jesus' compassion for "the lost sheep of the house of Israel" and for wayward disciples makes him like the good shepherd who leaves the ninety-nine on the hillside in order to search for one stray. He risks vulnerable, direct communication with people who need to repent, including the leaders who are plotting to have him crucified. He shares authority when he gives the disciples the power to bind and to loose and when he promises that God will answer their united prayers. Finally, he interprets his blood as a sign of forgiveness, which is offered to "many," meaning all who repent. Although the disciples fall far short of Jesus' expectations, he shows his forgiveness after the resurrection by calling them "brothers" and by trusting them to offer forgiveness to others. When we observe how Matthew portrays Jesus, there can be no doubt about how Matthew would answer the disciples' question in 18:1. Jesus is clearly the greatest in God's reign.

Furthermore, Matthew is eager to share Jesus' kind of greatness with others. Jesus tells the disciples to be like him (10:25), and he charges the Pharisees with hypocrisy because they do not practice what they teach (23:3). Therefore, it is almost essential for Matthew to show that Jesus obeys his own teaching. Indeed, Matthew's story is a powerful teaching tool because Jesus' words and actions reinforce one another so well. The audience hears about Jesus' example and then hears instructions on how to go and do likewise.

There is, however, a potential problem with telling readers to be like Jesus. The hero's example is so stellar and his commands so difficult that readers are likely to get discouraged. Jesus walks on water and is revealed as no less than the Son of God. How can we possibly measure up to that standard?

Perhaps we can find encouragement in the stories of present-day disciples who have tried with some success to follow Jesus' example and teaching. This book tells just a few such stories, but they are enough to show that discipleship according to Matthew 18 is not a thing of the past. Indeed, when Matthew 18 is interpreted as this book suggests, the potential applications are endless. Millions of stories about faithful discipleship could be told if only we were aware of them.

The authors of this book are deeply grateful for the examples of all the saints, sung and unsung, who show us what it means to follow Jesus faithfully. At the same time, we acknowledge again that good examples are not enough to save us. Following Jesus' example may seem as impossible for us as walking on water. We may also feel discouraged when we compare the successes of others with our more normal experiences.

In reality, our attempts to practice Matthew 18 usually have mixed results. Humble service and hospitality are not always a source of joy. Self-discipline sometimes fails, and so does compassion. Sisters and brothers often remain at odds with one another in spite of everyone's best attempts at centered communication and consensus-building. Unlimited forgiveness is easier to teach than to practice. While this book includes many positive examples, we have also tried to be realistic about human limitations, failures, and the need for grace.

Finding the Key

The key to faithful discipleship according to Matthew 18 is neither secret nor hidden, although it is sometimes lost or ignored. It is a life-giving relationship with the risen Jesus—the sort of relationship Jesus offers the disciples when he promises to be with them always. If Jesus were only a dead hero, his example and teachings would still challenge us, but he could not help us meet the challenges. We confess, however, that Jesus is alive and close at hand, which means that the help we need is always available. If we try to be like Jesus on our own strength, the result will be either pride or discouragement; but if we have a vital relationship with Jesus, he can shape us from the inside as we continue to focus our attention on him. Whatever Jesus asks of us is possible with his help. He understands our limitations, and he takes them into account as he calls us to serve in specific ways.

Matthew's accounts of the resurrection (28:1-20) and of Jesus walking on water (14:22-33) each bear witness to the importance of a life-giving relationship with Jesus. These accounts are similar in many ways. They each begin with a scene where Jesus apparently is absent. Then they reveal his presence as a living person with extraordinary power. Both accounts use a rare word meaning "doubt" or "hesitate" (14:31; 28:17), and both show Jesus responding to his followers' doubts with exactly the words and actions they need.

We have already noted that Peter's experience on the sea foreshadows his fearful denial of Jesus and his later restoration. Fortunately, Peter has an ongoing relationship with Jesus, whose power to save is at the forefront in both passages. Jesus knows Peter's limitations and abilities far better than Peter himself. Like a parent with a toddler, Jesus is there for him as he tries, falls, and tries again. Peter, meanwhile, has the faith to walk on water as long as his attention remains focused on Jesus. His failures come when he is distracted by the wind or by the unexpected arrest. When we read Matthew 14:22-33 and 28:1-20 together, they suggest that the disciples can follow Jesus' example in their post-Easter mission if, and only if, they remain focused on him.

It is especially important that both stories come to a climax with worship. Worship is the appropriate response to the powerful, loving presence of the One who transforms our hesitation and fear into hope and joy. In each story, worship comes to the disciples like a gift of new life, opening and preparing them for the tasks that lie ahead.

We are wise if worship is our first priority, just as it is the first priority for the disciples in 28:16-20. The only higher priority according to Matthew 5:24 is reconciliation with a sister or brother, but even then our goal is to worship in a reconciled community. Whenever we recognize Jesus, our tasks are clear: we need to adore him, to confess our faults, to listen for the word we need, and to ask what we should do next. Jesus' other priorities in 28:16-20 include discipling, baptizing, and teaching. Worship, however, comes first, perhaps so that it undergirds everything the disciples are called to do.

We need to set aside special times for worship, but we also need to let it permeate the whole fabric of our lives. If Jesus is with us always, there is no need to divide our lives into sacred and secular components. People who have a living relationship with Jesus can find him anywhere. Whenever co-workers at a factory reach a level of trust that they can speak about their deepest concerns, Jesus is the unseen listener. Official prayers are no longer recited in U.S. public schools, but Jesus is still there, and he hears the private, heartfelt prayers no one can ban. A pastor or deacon may go as Christ's representative to someone suffering in a hospital room and find that Jesus is already there. The volunteers at a soup kitchen know they cannot feed everyone who is hungry, not even all the neediest people in one city; nevertheless, for disciples who know that Jesus is present, the work of serving food can have meaning that extends far beyond its tiny impact on the worldwide problem of hunger. Each plateful can be a prayer that God will bless the recipient not only with a good meal, but with every other need. Each plateful is a prayer for the end of hunger and homelessness around the world. It is possible for Jesus' presence to fill our work, rest, and play so thoroughly that we never stop worshiping. Every moment of joyful gratitude is an act of praise. Every act of compassion is a prayer.[1]

Sunday worship services, for all their importance, are only a public dramatization of the constant worship that Jesus inspires and deserves. Therefore, at one level we agree with the people who say, "I don't need the church because I can worship Jesus anywhere." It *is* possible to worship Jesus anywhere; however, someone who does not worship regularly in church is not likely to do so on a golf course. We need the support of a faith community in order to learn and maintain the disciplines of worship. It is no coincidence that the promise in Matthew 18:20 is for those who *gather* in Jesus' name.

Of course, the church is full of imperfect people, as Matthew 18 also recognizes. It is easy to become discouraged with the weakness of the church, including the complacent routines that seem far removed from its real mission. When we are disappointed or even angry with the church, Jesus may be calling us first to examine ourselves and then to confront our sisters and brothers lovingly. The church needs prophets with the courage to challenge our complacency. Matthew 18 can show us how to be prophets within the church, but even prophets (*especially* prophets) need ways to deal faithfully with discouragement.

Again, Matthew's answer is a renewed relationship with Jesus. In Matthew 14:24-25, the disciples row most of the night into a headwind. The wind symbolizes the fierce opposition they face in their mission. The disciples are discouraged as well as terrified until they hear Jesus say, "Take heart, it is I; do not be afraid" (14:27). Similarly, Jesus keeps reminding us to take heart because he is near.

Although we are rightly concerned about the future of the world and the church, we can rejoice that their future does not depend on us. God works through all kinds of circumstances, and God's reign finally will be established on earth. God gives us the privilege of helping in that great endeavor, but God will find ways to accomplish it with or without our help. We do not need to be discouraged as if we were responsible for making history come out right. Furthermore, the death and resurrection of Jesus shows that God can take a disaster, humanly speaking, and turn it into an enormous good. Consequently, we have reason to trust that the risen Jesus will lead us as promised through our own experiences of death and resurrection. We can rejoice in the midst of all kinds of circumstances because we know that our Beloved is near.

If a living relationship with Jesus can overcome discouragement, it can also transform pride. When our attention is focused on Jesus, we cannot help noticing that our virtues are quite shabby compared with his. We may be tempted to avoid a relationship with Jesus precisely because he is a threat to our pride. Jesus, however, is not trying to shame us but to rescue us. In Matthew's story, Peter often looks like a fool in comparison with Jesus, but when Peter finally recognizes his need for help, Jesus is there to lift him up. Something similar happens whenever we accept the grace Jesus offers. His grace leaves no room for pride, but that is a small price to pay for the privilege of being children in God's household.

The key to Christian discipleship is experiencing God's grace through a life-giving relationship with Jesus. That relationship challenges and empowers us to share grace with others. As we become more deeply rooted in Christ, our discipleship according to Matthew 18 can flourish. We can become channels of God's grace, eager to seek, welcome, and forgive the people whom God wants to love through us.

Questions for Discussion

1. Take some time now to review what you have learned through this study. How has your interpretation of the Gospel of Matthew

and of Matthew 18 changed? What contemporary stories of discipleship stand out for you, and what have you learned from them? If you attempted one or more of the "story starter" projects, what did you learn from that experience?

2. How do you respond when someone lifts up the heroic actions of others as an example for you to follow? Are you inspired to "go and do likewise," or discouraged with thoughts that you could never measure up? Do you agree with the authors that good examples are not enough to save us?

3. The authors suggest that the key to faithful discipleship according to Matthew 18 is "a life-giving relationship with the risen Jesus." Do you agree? What does "a life-giving relationship with Jesus" mean for you?

4. Can you identify with Peter's experience of being rescued by Jesus? If so, when and how were you rescued?

5. How do you understand the relationship between Sunday worship services and worship throughout the week? Do you agree with the authors that we need to let worship "permeate the whole fabric of our lives"? How might you practice that vision more fully?

6. How does Jesus help you deal with discouragement? with pride?

NOTES

1. Theodore W. Jennings, Jr., *Life as Worship: Prayer and Praise in Jesus' Name* (Grand Rapids: Eerdmans, 1982), 80, 115-119.